"Debra M. Amidon has captured the most forward-thinking ideas in the areas of knowledge management and learning organizations and their impact on innovation. These emerging concepts are effectively and creatively linked together and paint a clear picture of the possibilities of the future." —**Gordon P. Petrash**, Global Director, Intellectual Asset & Capital Management, The Dow Chemical Company

"Just when you think you've caught up with the latest in strategic management theory, along comes Debra Amidon to challenge you with new and more exciting possibilities. This book is not intended for the neophyte manager. It is a mind-stretcher for the experienced and sophisticated manager whose corporation expects him or her to keep them well ahead of the competition." —**Dr. A.R.C. Westwood**, Former V.P., Research and Technology, Sandia National Laboratories and Martin Marietta Corporation

"This seminal book places a laser-beam focus on the most important core competency of our time—innovation—and stresses the need for the development of solid metrics to measure its performance." —**Dr. Corey Carbonara**, Vice President for Innovation, Baylor University

"The knowledge revolution, which we all are experiencing in our own ways, demands a different approach to, attitude toward, and implementation of our management systems—be they in industry, government, or academia. This book deals with these complex issues in a stimulating and thorough way." —**Dr. Erich Bloch**, Distinguished Fellow, Council on Competitiveness (Washington, DC)

"If you would like to know how to participate in and be part of the fourth wave that is coming, your company has to learn how to innovate as an organization. Debra shows you the way to achieve that creative use of the knowledge that exists in the minds of your people so that you can redefine your company to be part of the fourth wave." —**Robert H. Buckman**, President and CEO, Buckman Laboratories

"This book should be a wake-up call to small companies, as well as large, if they expect to compete in today's world. Although leaders of small organizations may think that they don't have the resources to pursue knowledge innovation, in fact they have the perfect laboratories for applying Ms. Amidon's strategies. Small companies have the agility, focus, ease of communication, and flexible culture that simplify the implementation of innovation management. Moreover, the supplier and customer alliances that are essential to survival can be readily shaped into a virtual enterprise, or Strategic Business Network, to provide competitive advantage." —**Dr. Robert Levy**, Energy BioSystems Corporation

"Think about Monet's series paintings—it's the changing context that gives them meaning and significance, just as context gives knowledge meaning and significance. We all need a *Ken* awakening!" —**Dr. Tony Brewer**, Wentworth Company (England)

"'Ken you?' While this book is not a "Ken-do" management text, it is provocative and does evoke a *Ken* awakening. After reading Amidon's book, you will not be complacent. You will want to move rapidly from an information—and even knowledge source—to one of wisdom. Some people learn to live; innovators live to learn. For the latter, this book should be on their must-read list." —**Dr. F. Timothy Janis**, President, ARAC, former Executive Director, Technology Transfer Society

"This book provides a sparkling synthesis of emergent knowledge management practices. Debra Amidon brings clarity and focus to the application of knowledge for product and service innovation. An intriguing read for any organization developing knowledge and innovation strategy." —**Verna Allee**, author, *The Knowledge Evolution*

"The ability to create good metaphors and analogies (and tell good stories) is critical to the success of a theorist in this emerging field. Amidon's Monet metaphor is powerful." —**Britton Manasco**, editor and publisher, *Knowledge Inc.*

"When entering uncharted territory it is wise to rely on the guidance of a pioneer explorer. As an early protagonist, Debra Amidon has mastered the elusive concepts of knowledge management. She will introduce you to the intricacies of the emerging economy of knowledge with ease and confidence. If you are looking for a book that gives you a clear picture of knowledge innovation and helps you diagnose your potential and set your own strategy to survive the knowledge imperative, this is it!" —**Dr. Francisco J. Carrillo**, Director, Center for Knowledge Systems, ITESM (Mexico)

"The power of innovation is one of the most fundamental resources for both organization and societal wealth. Ms. Amidon offers insightful and practical hands-on suggestions of how to move ahead with a powerful process for *your* knowledge innovation." —**Leif Edvinsson**, from the Foreword

"This adds up to far more than a timely review of the forces shaping tomorrow's business. It provides senior managers with a framework to take advantage of what is perhaps their organization's most precious, but under-managed, resource: knowledge. Everyone reading this book can expect to be rewarded with a new and stimulating vision of how their businesses should be run." —**David Harvey**, Director, Business Intelligence (England)

"Exceptionally skilled in building consensus and working on complex issues that require collaborative efforts...with a rare quality of sensitivity and resoluteness." —**Dr. George Kozmetsky**, Founder, Teledyne Corporation

"Ms. Amidon displays extensive knowledge of technology transfer. She is articulate and effective in communication of complex ideas and concepts to diverse audiences." —**Larry W. Sumney**, President and CEO, Semiconductor Research Corporation

"On my wall is a poster of Monet's 'The Water Lily Pond' showing the bridge at Giverny. I look at it to inspire me when I'm planning for the future. Debra's book has the same effect—it's an excellent bridge between tomorrow and today, and between theory and practice." —**Dr. David J. Skyrme**, editor, *I³: Intelligence, Insight, and Innovation*

"Today's world is in the whirl of accelerated change in all domains. Old theories and foundations are dying and the new are not yet invented. Management leaders are living in the dark as to what strategies will make them successful. Exclusive focus on the short term does not enable a vision of the future. Debra's book provides the strategic light with a theory of modern management, precise methods for application, and a formula for building the successful knowledge-based enterprise." —**Dr. Eunika Mercier-Laurent**, EML Conseil-Knowledge Management (France)

"At Monsanto, the challenge that we have taken upon ourselves is 'How do we engage the collective intellect of the people in Monsanto to turn information into insight to serve our customers and the marketplace?' Debra M. Amidon lucidly explores the concept of knowledge innovation and its criticality for 'the success of an enterprise, vitality of a nation's economy, and the advancement of society.' I highly recommend the book." —**Bipin Junnarkar**, Director, Knowledge Management, Monsanto Company

"As Debra suggests, the innovation process must be made explicit. In this respect, her innovation assessment questions raise many of the issues we have found to be most important. This is one way to get at how knowledge is applied rather than accumulated." —**Dr. Bruce Wright**, Director, Office of Innovation, Hoechst-Celanese

"Debra Amidon has taken important steps to create clarity in the world of real-time changes and multidimensional cooperation. Her book offers a powerful managerial thinking base that will be essential for the future of business." —**Rauno Puskala**, CEO, Synertek Oy (Finland)

"Our organizations and our ways of thinking are changing so fast that we need more than new tools...we need new insights and new mental processes. Debra Amidon's book is a great beginning for those who must not just manage change but must conceptualize new organizational designs that stimulate change and adaptation so naturally that they are almost unnoticed." —**Dr. Michael Crow**, Vice Provost, Columbia University

"Debra is at the leading edge—or, as she occasionally says, the 'bleeding edge'—of thought regarding innovation and the transforming power of knowledge to lead enterprises successfully into the twenty-first century. She exhibits an uncanny ability to tease the best conceptual thinking out of individuals fortunate enough to work with her. Her advice and encouragement have been absolutely central to the transformation of corporate relations at MIT." —**Tom Moebus**, Director, Corporate Relations, Massachusetts Institute of Technology

"Debra Amidon is the first visionary cartographer of knowledge innovation. With her book, managers will find their way across this complex new terrain, which is critical to success in the twenty-first century." —**Jessica Lipnack** and **Jeffrey Stamps**, Co-founders, The Networking Institute, co-authors, *Virtual Teams*

"What is the why of intellectual capital and knowledge management, if it is not to create vibrant and innovative companies. Debra Amidon writes with passion, insight, and foresight as she makes accessible the exciting new field of knowledge innovation." —**Dr. Charles M. Savage**, author, *Fifth Generation Management: Co-creating Through Virtual Enterprising, Dynamic Teaming, and Knowledge Networking*

"Both insightful and entertaining. Debra M. Amidon has created an indispensable guide to management in the new, dynamic knowledge economy." —**Dr. Kenneth Preiss**, Senior Fellow, Agility Forum, coauthor, *Cooperate to Compete: Building Agile Business Relationships*

"Debra's perspective on knowledge management is compelling and can be compared to Monet's perspective on painting—understanding requires the big view in order to see the detail. Her ideas more than work—they win!" —**Dr. Bill Miller**, VP, Research and Business Development, Steelcase North America

"The richness of these ideas and concepts is challenging—especially in their implications. It's not *what* you know. It's not even *who* you know that is all important. Instead, Debra Amidon demonstrates that it is *how* you know—how the innovation process can be made to function for your own business success." —**Dr. Parry Norling**, Planning Director, DuPont

"This book is a call to concentrate on the core of innovation. Its vision will urge you to act by participating in the international network of knowledge management practitioners." —**Dr. Jean Marc Le Duc**, Direction Generale, Ministere de la Recherché et de l'Espace (France)

"Debra Amidon is the most original conceptual thinker I have come across in the area of knowledge management. Her ideas and concepts in this book are far reaching and form a powerful foundation for research and practice in the years to come. It is a gold mine!" —**Dr. Karl Erik Sveiby**, author, *The New Organizational Wealth: Managing and Measuring Knowledge Based Assets* (Australia)

"As global networks accelerate the pace of business innovation, the biggest challenge facing business leaders today is managing the explosion in corporate knowledge. This book provides a robust framework for managing the people, processes, networks, and business models underlying a company's knowledge base. In the twenty-first century, business leaders have a stark choice: either manage their knowledge effectively or face extinction." —**Sheridan Tatsuno**, author, *Created in Japan,* President, Dreamscape Productions

"Debra Amidon has provided a much-needed blueprint for how knowledge might be managed systematically, effectively, and profitably. This book points to how management of knowledge is central to continued innovation." —**Dr. Karl Wiig**, Chairman & CEO, Knowledge Research Institute, Inc.

"Debra Amidon knows how to help organizations design for knowledge."—**Julie Anixter**, VP, Learning Systems, Anixter, Inc.

"If you have reached a point where you believe that it is essential to tap into the full potential of knowledge in your organization, very few can offer better advice than Debra Amidon. Based on more than a decade of experience in applying insights on knowledge-driven innovation to the reality of business, she offers practical, impactful, and systematic ways to partner with your customers in order to create whole new pathways of value creation."—**Hubert Saint-Onge**, VP, People, Knowledge, and Strategies, The Mutual Group (Canada)

INNOVATION STRATEGY FOR THE KNOWLEDGE ECONOMY

INNOVATION STRATEGY FOR THE KNOWLEDGE ECONOMY

The *Ken* Awakening

DEBRA M. AMIDON

Butterworth-Heinemann

Boston • Oxford • Johannesburg
Melbourne • New Delhi • Singapore

Butterworth–Heinemann

A member of the Reed Elsevier group

Recognizing the importance of preserving what has been written, Butterworth-Heinemann prints its books on acid-free paper whenever possible.

Butterworth–Heinemann supports the efforts of American Forests and the Global ReLeaf program in its campaign for the betterment of trees, forests, and our environment.

Library of Congress Cataloging-in-Publication Data

Amidon, Debra M., 1946-
Innovation strategy for the knowledge economy: the ken awakening / Debra M. Amidon.
p. cm.
Includes bibliographical references and index.
ISBN 0-7506-9841-1 (alk. paper)
1. Creative ability in business. 2. Management. I. Title.
HD53.A46 1997
658.4—dc21 96-52396
CIP

British Library Cataloguing-in-Publication Data
A catalogue record for this book is available from the British Library.

The publisher offers special discounts on bulk orders of this book. For information, please contact:

Manager of Special Sales
Butterworth-Heinemann
313 Washington Street
Newton, MA 02158-1626
Tel: 617-928-2500
Fax: 617-928-2620

For information on all business publications available, contact our World Wide Web home page at: http://www.bh.com/bb

10 9 8 7 6 5 4 3 2 1

Printed in the United States of America

To all those
who have touched me
and from whom
I have grown—
especially Kendra and Clint

About the Cover

This computer-enhanced photograph of Giverny, France, captures the impressionist style of Monet's garden paintings. The original photograph, taken by Debra M. Amidon, won first place at the Deerfield Country Fair, New Hampshire. In his final years, Claude Monet exceeded the boundaries of what anyone would have thought possible. His masterpieces are a vision of courage. They represent the same bold vision we must establish in order to capitalize on opportunities present in an interdependent global economy.

Contents

Foreword

The power of innovation is one of the most fundamental resources for both organization and societal wealth. The power of innovation creates value for its stakeholders. The power of innovation is found in the intellectual capital border zone between human capital and structural capital. The power of innovation is achieved as a multiplicative effect by rapid knowledge sharing and evolving new applications. The critical success factor is not only the number of new ideas, but more so, their implementation. This is achieved through the systematic, explicit approach outlined in this book.

As Debra M. Amidon suggests, *yesterday's theory is today's essential management practice*. Developing new theory around knowledge innovation is consequently very commendable. This has many similarities to the work in progress at Skandia Insurance Company, Ltd. related to intellectual capital. Both approaches aim to develop ways to nurture the roots of sustainability and to outline a broader and deepening perspective of innovation. One can see an analogy with the development of Impressionist art, in that Claude Monet provided a new perspective of painting. This view is consistent with one of the dimensions mentioned by Professor Gary Hamel, London Business School, who says that *perspective is worth fifty IQ points*. The implication is that to be able to reach a degree of smartness or intelligence, it is necessary to take the broader perspective and see the system in its entirety.

Looking at the increasing level of learning, as well as the increasing degree of complexity, it becomes evident that the compression of time is fundamental to the aspects of knowledge innovation. This collapse of time has been noticed, among others, by D. W. Hock, founder and CEO Emeritus of Visa. Because of the shortening cycle time, development and launching of new media, technologies, and scientific discoveries are ever increasing. However, the launching of new organizational architecture and behavior has lagged behind. Thus, there is a need for innovative approaches to turn the future into an asset. It is a matter of viewing the future as an opportunity to develop products and services. Simultaneously, the company envisions the opportunity to develop new partnering relationships with customers and stakeholders. Together we move forward.

Skandia views the concept of knowledge innovation as a process of optimizing the flow of competencies within the group and its multiple networks in operating environments. The objective is to enhance success and prosperity for all parties involved. This requires the development of work methods and techniques for collective knowledge handling with a focus on organizational capital. Awareness of available knowledge and the rapid sharing of knowledge are central factors.

This work method can be described as a progression on the life cycle curve developed by Charles Handy. (Note: See chapter 1.) This shows a gradual evolution in which the challenge is to successfully move to the second curve. The velocity of movement along the first development curve and the ability to advance to the next level of the second curve may be called organizational float—the balance between multiple and sometimes seemingly opposing forces. It may become the most central organizational competence for strategic success and survival in the twenty-first century. It can be described as making waves of innovation in organizations and then riding them into the future. The future can then be viewed as an ocean of unexploited opportunities.

This process of turning the future into an asset could also be described as a process beyond scenario or future planning. It might be described as a process of *futurizing,* which implies the grasping of opportunities and making continuous waves of similar sigmoid curves. The number of such continuous waves might be seen as the new enterprise DNA pattern for continuous knowledge innovation—the balance of incremental and quantum change in endless evolution.

This book is about the evolution of the *ken*—the core of knowledge innovation. One of the dimensions of ken is to offer a chance for reflection and contemplation before taking further action. This book affords such an opportunity. It offers executives the chance to take a quantum leadership approach to see the whole perspective while, at the same time, managing the finer details with a systematic step-by-step process for innovation assessment and knowledge innovation development.

By availing themselves of such opportunities, organizations can add to their institutional change and continuous renewal process. This is one of the more fundamental dimensions for the systematic usage of intellectual resources and adding to value creation. Besides describing the theory of development and providing interesting information concerning contributors to the new knowledge economy, this book constitutes a milestone in the comprehensive work of Renewal and Development—a modern view of R&D management. From the Skandia perspective, it has been one of the corner building blocks for our intellectual development. Through her book, Ms. Amidon offers insightful and practical hands-on suggestions of how to move ahead with a powerful process for your knowledge innovation.

Leif Edvinsson
Vice President of Intellectual Capital
and Director of Skandia Futures Centers

7 October 1996
Stockholm, Sweden

Preface

What began for me in 1987 with the roundtable "Managing the Knowledge Asset into the 21st Century" has become an active community of knowledge practice in which it is a privilege to participate. A critical mass of professionals are creating a future previously unimaginable. It is based on modern learning theory, the nature of complementary competencies, and best global management practices.

This book is intended for managers who have practiced the best quality and reengineering management techniques and are ready to transform their organizations with the systematic notions of knowledge creation and application. It is for organization leaders who prefer to be inspired with innovation strategy than hit over the head with change management techniques. It does not deal with barriers, hurdles, or conflicts to be resolved, but rather paints a possible vision of how we can take advantage of our collective learnings to move an enterprise forward.

There are few quick fixes in this field because the changes are so fundamental. On the other hand, there are ways to be introduced to the core concepts and get ideas on how they might readily be applied within your organization…today. For those who only want suggestions for how to begin, I suggest that you scan the preface and the opening chapter and then skip to the innovation assessment outlined in chapters 5, 7, and 8. For those who would like to understand the rationale for such an innovation focus based on the flow of intellectual capital, chapters 2, 4, and 6 will be useful. For others who are ready to embrace the journey and trace their own roots and vision, most of the contents of the book should be of some value.

In 1991, Peter Drucker reviewed the presentation "Creating a Global Innovation Management System," which I gave at the Grande Colloque de Perspective in Lyons, France. He wrote that he liked it and "learned from it." Years later, I shared some of the newer material on innovation strategy with him, and his written response was "Debra, you are way beyond my *ken*." Not being familiar with the word, I referred to the dictionary to discover the real power in the term—integrating simultaneously a perspective based on careful observation and a range of vision.

The genesis for the book formed.

The term "ken" has provided a focus for this work as there has been a flourish of activity—books, conferences, trade press articles—on the subject of knowledge management. Thousands of executives now carry the word "knowledge" in their title and job responsibilities. Many have written that these ideas are likely to go the way of other management fads. Consulting firms have initiated new practices in the area, some of which have evolved without the practitioners' having any understanding of the theories underpinning this new notion. They think that substituting the term "knowledge" for existing information bases and methodologies is the quick way to their own revenue growth. For those who do understand—and you probably wouldn't be reading this book if you didn't—there is an awakening that we are at a cathartic moment in the evolution of modern management. The transformation is fundamental; and we are all playing a role in its birth.

In *Webster's New World Dictionary: Second College Edition*, the word *ken* is defined as both a noun and a verb:

> ***ken*** (ken) v. 1. To know (a person or thing). 2. To recognize. 3. To descry (i.e., discern something difficult to catch sight of; discover through careful observation or investigation); to have an understanding of something.
>
> n. 1. Perception; understanding. 2.a. Range of vision. b. View; sight; to make known.

Not only is this the ideal term to synthesize the knowledge management movement, it integrates history and vision, respects the difficulty in discovering the unknown, and paints the picture of perspective. It helps us appreciate the difficulty in discerning our roots as well as the value of envisioning a future that may not exist today. It is the unifying concept to catapult this "community of knowledge practice" forward.

Moreover, it has international implications to transcend cultural barriers. *Ken* is I Ching, the ancient Chinese system for divining the future, which means "stillness." It indicates that now is the time to find quiet and strength in silence...the need for inner peace...end the babbling of the mind...confront situations with equanimity. Given all the activity inherent in change management, perhaps many organizations need a chance for reflection and contemplation before further action. This may appear impossible amid the currents of activity that consume our most precious resources—time and mind.

Ken also has German, Scottish, Celtic, and Dutch roots. *Kennen* means "to know." *Kennis* is "knowledge" or "acquaintance," and *kenner* is "connoisseur" or "someone who has knowledge." *Kenn-nummer* means "reference number." *Kendra* is Welsh for "all-knowing woman" and Sanskrit for "center." All these terms have meaning for this emerging community of knowledge practice, which demands an understanding of the unknown. It legitimizes not having all the answers, but venturing forth with what may be known. In the Japanese context, *ken* equals *katana* equals "sword," the most important possession of the Samurai. This symbol is for the sacred spirit or soul, and only a few katana warriors are alive today.

We no longer live in an "either/or" world. We must learn to continually balance seeming opposites—long and short term; roots and vision; change and stability; theory and practice. In the 1980s we applied research methods to create a managerial architecture and standards with the same technical rigor as we developed technical architectures and standards. Thanks to the lead *ken* pioneers, we are able to provide specific examples of how these concepts are employed in day-to-day operational strategies.

Treat this book as a compass for your journey into the new territory of knowledge systems. It does not provide all the answers, but asks some of the right questions. Interdependencies are built into the assessment tools by design, because organizations can no longer survive with traditional competitive strategies. The world is transforming at a more rapid rate than we can even comprehend. The dramatic changes of the last decade may seem trivial in comparison to what lies ahead. Success in the future will depend more than ever on coherence and the harnessing of complementary competencies to enable the optimal flow of knowledge.

In chapter 1, there is a description of the managerial *Awakening,* which dawns with the turn of the century. Chapter 2—*Kaleidoscopic*

Dynamics—provides an introduction to the myriad changes we are undergoing and defines the management challenge of the next millennium. Chapter 3 introduces a way to view the evolution of the movement through *Wellsprings Timelines* and a technique for managers to trace their own perspective. Chapter 4 describes the emerging *Community of Knowledge Practice,* suggesting that innovation strategy may be the binding force to create a compelling vision for sustainability. Chapter 5 outlines the *Innovation Value System* (as opposed to traditional value-chain methodologies) as a means to create the optimal flow of knowledge across traditional organizational boundaries. Chapter 6 outlines a *Management Architecture* and describes how some companies have adopted the elements and created benchmarking capabilities to monitor best knowledge management practices. Chapters 7 and 8 detail the modules of an *Innovation Assessment Tool* designed to create a series of integrated initiatives across the enterprise, ranging from coordination of the process to utilization of the cyberspace. Chapter 9 focuses on *Customers* as a source of knowledge and innovative partnering techniques for optimal interaction. Finally, chapter 10 summarizes emerging modern managerial standards and outlines a *Prospectus for the Future.*

The architecture, standards, and modules for innovation strategy are based on years of management research in both industrial and academic settings. Materials were designed to be universal in scope and transcend any function, sector, industry, or geography. They have been tested in national and international forums with representatives from North, Central, and South America, Eastern and Western Europe, Asia, Australia, Russia, and developing nations around the world. The Entovation Network is composed of more than seventeen hundred theorists and practitioners linking forty-four countries. They participate in a variety of electronic and face-to-face professional forums dedicated to advancing the state of the art and the state of the practice simultaneously.

In his final years, Claude Monet advanced well beyond the boundaries of what anyone would have thought possible. His gardens at Giverny are breathtaking and his masterpieces now featured in L'Orangerie are a spectacle of courage. They represent the same kind of bold vision we must establish to capitalize on the unleashed opportunities present in an interdependent global economy.

This book provides the reader with a sound, practical framework for instituting innovation strategy beyond the traditional definition of flow of parts or finances. At the core is an understanding of the dual value of *knowledge* (content) and *innovation* (process) using *"real-time" learning* as the methodology. Peter Drucker says that you need only one competence for the future: *innovation* and the ability to measure performance. This book offers a framework in which to crystallize your direction.

Let me know of your own progress.

Always in your network,

Debra

June 1996

E-mail: debra@entovation.com
URL: http://www.entovation.com

Acknowledgments

The **Entovation Network** is composed of more than seventeen hundred theorists and practitioners in forty-four countries. They participate in a variety of electronic and professional forums dedicated to advancing the state of the *art* and the state of the *practice* simultaneously. It is their insight from which I learn daily.

There are three mentors, in particular, to whom I am indebted for motivating me to share my expertise in print. **Dr. Erich Bloch** represents the ultimate practitioner, serving as an IBM executive, as the director of the National Science Foundation, and finally as a distinguished fellow on the Council on Competitiveness. **Dr. George Kozmetsky**, founder of Teledyne and the IC^2 Institute at the University of Texas, is the person who first opened my eyes to the prospects of innovation strategy. **Dr. A. R. C. Westwood** is the ultimate innovator, having served in leadership positions with Martin Marietta, Sandia National Laboratory, the Industrial Research Institute, and the National Research Council. They are all national treasures and international statesmen. Over the years, they have been my inspiration and the thoughtful coaches of my practice. They believed in me when I wondered if the frontier was worth exploring. It has been my privilege to know them personally.

There are several Entovation Fellows who have contributed substantively to the content and processes espoused in the book: **Francis V. Alla; Dr. Sean and Katherine Gadman; Carille Greenberg; Pat Kulesz; Jessica Lipnack; Dr. Eunika Mercier-Laurent; Laurel Rans; Larraine Segil, Esq.; Dr. David Skyrme; Jeffrey Stamps; Dr. Karl Erik**

Sveiby; and Larry Todd Wilson. We have realized that our interdependent businesses are always works in progress in the constant state of redesign. Together, we hope to create the next generation of management technology.

Finally, there are other Entovation colleagues and clients who continue to be a source of my own learning, such as **Dr. Christopher Bart; Dr. Bob Buckman; Dr. Corey Carbonara; Dr. Francisco J. Carrillo; Dr. Michael M. Crow; Dr. Gale Cutler; Leif Edvinsson; Dr. David Harvey; Dr. Tim Janis; Dr. Jean Marc Le Duc; Dr. Bob Levy; Meredith Malmberg; Britton Manasco; Dr. William Miller; Tom Moebus; Kay Mosby; Brian (BO) Newman; Dr. Parry Norling; Dr. Ken Preiss; Rauno Puskala; Dr. Bernard Reverdy; Dr. Charles Savage; Dr. Ed Schein; Dr. Ron Smart; Adrian Smith; Dr. Michael Smith; Dr. William Spencer; Hubert St. Onge; Dr. Ray Stata; Larry Sumney; Sheridan Tatsuno; Bob Wiele; Dr. Karl Wiig; E.J. Witterholt; Tom Wojcik; Elizabeth Wolfson**, and many, many more.

Last, but certainly not least, is the capable staff of Butterworth-Heinemann, especially **Stephanie Gelman, Hilary Selby Polk,** and **Karen Speerstra**, who was introduced to me as "the midwife of ideas before their time." I am indebted to them for their constant care, insight, and advice on how to leverage this work.

Rarely do professionals have such an opportunity to recognize those who have been so instrumental in their careers, including family, such as Mom Amidon, Aunt Barbara, Uncle "Joe," Joan, and, of course, Clint and Kendra. As I reflect on how each person has touched my life, I am reminded of the kaleidoscope of images...constantly changing...adding new dimensions to my thinking...reminding me of the wonders available when living a dream.

1

A Bold Awakening

Just as the Lotus grows
up from the darkness of the mud
to the surface of the water,
opening its blossom only after it has raised itself beyond the surface,
and remains unsullied from both earth and water, which nourished it—
in the same way the mind,
born in the human body,
unfolds its true qualities ("petals")
after it has raised itself beyond the turbid floods of passion and ignorance,
and transforms the dark powers of the depths
into the radiantly pure nectar of Enlightenment-consciousness.
—GOVINDA[1]

We had been to Paris several times—my daughter and I. In 1989, we decided to take a side trip to Giverny. Claude Monet had always been my favorite artist, but I never understood why…until now. We were experiencing dramatic changes in our lives; and the gardens—flourishing in the afternoon sun—were inspiring. We picked up petals from the ground and took them home to remember the beauty of the day and the moment. We began to dream again.

The same year, I had graduated from the Massachusetts Institute of Technology as an Alfred Sloan Fellow—learning with some of the best managers in the world representing twenty-four countries. In our orientation, we shared our mutual aspirations for harmony in our personal and professional lives. In my thesis, *Global Innovation Strategy: Creating Value-Added Alliances,*[2] I created a "lotus innovation flower" with intersecting petals to depict the multiple interconnections needed for business success in the emerging dynamic global economy. It was clear we had much to learn from one another—Eastern and Western cultures alike.

My focus had always been on education and the implementation of new ideas. In the 1960s, we were activists. In the 1970s, we were described as change agents. In the 1980s, we became strategists, envisioning a future others may not yet see. Today, we are the architects of transformation, pioneering a future based on collaborative—not competitive—strategy.

Something fundamental has happened along the way. Boundaries have virtually disappeared. We witnessed the end of the Cold War, a new appreciation for the value of diversity, dramatic changes in the way we work, and the emergence of a networked society accelerated by computer and communications technology. Indeed, there is a renewed understanding of the importance of the human element in business operations and the inevitable nature of natural evolution.

It wasn't until years later that I learned about Sarasvati, the goddess of knowledge, who stands in a lotus flower. Nor was I familiar with her companion, Lakshmi, the goddess of wealth, and the integral connection between the two. For thirty years, I have worked in the arena of connections; the past ten have been dedicated to a focus on intellectual wealth—for the success of an enterprise, the vitality of a nation's economy, and the well-being of society as a whole.

The world has been ravished by a plague that has shattered the very foundation of our dream—that hard work and a good education will ensure a stable standard of living. Instead, hundreds of thousands find themselves unemployed—and unemployable—by the downside of quality, reengineering, and "right-sizing" initiatives. In many respects, creativity and responsible risk-taking have been squeezed out of the system. Organizations find themselves left with rigid, constrained hierarchical leaders who are unaccustomed to the beauty of fluid, empowered organizational forms that are able to capitalize on business opportunities as they arise. When the enterprise is viewed from an intellectual perspective, knowledge resides in every human being in the system. How they spend their time, learn from their interactions, and feed ideas forward to improve operations is fundamental to business viability. In short, it is innovation capability that now provides the distinctive competencies of a successful enterprise.

As my daughter prepared her major school project on Claude Monet, her conclusion was that "he had the courage to be different." When I asked her what that meant, she described how the artists who preceded him painted pictures that required you to look closely at the canvas to see the detail. Monet—and the other Impressionists—painted in a way that required you to step back in order to see the detail. It is essential to see the whole and the interrelationships of color, texture, and mood to appreciate a work.

Similarly, we are at a juncture in the era of business management in which the traditional Alfred Sloan and Tayloristic methods can no longer cope with the exploding opportunities afforded in a global economy in rapid transition. Enterprises across all the sectors have experienced excruciating cost-cutting and productivity measures that have not taken into account the real value of the intellectual capability required to excel. Managers are now seeking progressive ways to ensure that creativity and innovation are nurtured in the future.

Whether we think in terms of lotus flowers or water lilies, we are witnessing a blossoming fed by several streams of activity that I call "emerging communities of knowledge practice." People at every managerial level are discovering new modes of interaction that promote continual "real-time" learning. Indeed, a consciousness is emerging from the depths of the darkness.

Managing in the "World Trade of Ideas"

Yesterday's theory is today's essential management practice. What was considered theoretical, strategic, or visionary only a few years ago is now considered fundamental to the survival of today's enterprises. We live in a world in which the application of new ideas may be the primary competitive advantage. Change is the only constant, and learning to embrace and ride those dynamics requires substantially different management practices.

To deal with yesterday's complexity, Alfred Sloan developed methods to separate businesses into manageable pieces, such as *strategic business units* (SBUs). This was not inconsistent with the industrialization techniques established by Frederick Taylor, who separated manufacturing processes into linear mechanized tasks to enable mass production. It was natural that the concepts of a value chain developed by Michael E. Porter, Harvard University, would be expanded to include all functions of the innovation process from idea creation to practical application. Indeed, this notion of dividing the discrete parts into components that could be well defined, understood, and managed was to serve businesses well.

In the 1980s, something dramatic happened. The rules of business management changed overnight. The world blossomed as a whole. While business opportunities seemed inexhaustible, so did the intensification of global competition. Complexity was increased by the acceleration of technological change and the rapid acceptance of computer and electronic communications. Markets shaped and reshaped as niche-market vendors capitalized on connecting products, services, and businesses in ways unimagined a few years earlier. Larger companies experimented with radical diversification and alliances of all forms, including those with archrival competitors. The notions of independent, competitive strategies—although still prominent in government rhetoric—were being diluted by the intense need to cooperate in order to survive.

As we approach the next millennium, we find ourselves—as individuals, groups, organizations, and nations—rethinking the way we interact. Instead of analyzing barriers, we are seeking common ground for action. Instead of focusing on conflict resolution, we are defining new ways of learning with one another so that we may define a better future for us all. This is reflected in many of the current managerial practices today, such as teaming, networking, and action learning. We are realizing the true value of an individual within the organization and how that human talent can best be harnessed to sustain the profitable growth of the enterprise and the individual.

In part, we must thank the pioneers in the "soft sciences" who have continually reminded us that organizations are composed of humans—developing and interacting with one another—in the course of their daily work. We realize that the negative effects of Taylorism are not conducive to thriving in a dynamic economy in which the variables change and are affected by change like a kaleidoscope. No longer can mechanistic, linear management strategies survive. In fact, strategic planning as a profession has undergone a dramatic transformation. Strategy is now a matter of leadership more than plans, the ability to inspire vision more than to articulate it, and the notion of sustained movement over time more than financial short-term successes.

Perhaps this has always been the case, but we were at a loss for how to manage such intangibles effectively. Now that business leaders have realized the value of intellectual capital, they are struggling for ways to represent it on the balance sheet as an asset, not a liability. If they cannot define it, it cannot be properly measured, monitored, and/or enhanced. Knowledge is a significantly unique attribute when viewed from the perspective of the individual, the team, or the organization as a whole. Gaining knowledge is a human process dealing with mental objects, requiring awareness and intuition, and is transferable only through learning. Information, on the other hand, is easily transferable, represented in physical objects, and reproducible at a low cost. No wonder executives are having difficulty shifting their orientation to knowledge-intensive environments at the same time that they are mandated to produce significant cost-savings through quality, downsizing, and other productivity measures.

Simultaneously, the walls have come down—between nations, between industries, between sectors of the economy, and between functions of an organization. Boundaries are fading and symbiosis is the priority of the day. There is a new respect for the value of the whole and an appreciation for the role one can play to affect the outcome. If we step back and envision the entire innovation system, we get a better sense of the interrelationships of the parts. Rather than a focus on discrete functions (e.g., Finance, Human Resources, Information Technology, R&D, Manufacturing, Marketing, Sales, and Service, etc.), we have a picture of how one contributes to the other. Through initiatives such as simultaneous development processes, concurrent engineering, agile manufacturing, et al., enterprises are realizing the value of the interdependencies rather than the differences in orientation.

Transform While Successful

Where do we turn to find guidance in a world filled with uncertainty, complexity, and interdependencies? This is new territory, and we are still reeling from the effects of rigorous quality and reengineering efforts, which—even when successfully implemented—have left organizations too lean to innovate. New ideas need nurturing, and the leaders who create them must be rewarded for responsible risk-taking. Many current environments, however, have become unforgiving of "mistakes" and reluctant to experiment with new modes of operation precisely at the same time that the market economy is demanding novel approaches.

Most organizations have been heavily vested in quality, reengineering, and change management strategies over the past decade. Although significant benefits have been reaped, the reality is that many enterprises are finding themselves at a loss for how next to proceed. In fact, there is real evidence that all the "right-sizing" strategies may be having the reverse effect of what is needed for twenty-first-century competition.

We need not belabor the point that many organizations have not reaped the performance results anticipated from their significant investment in quality and reengineering efforts. Productivity gains seem to be offset by the rapidly changing dynamics in the competitive marketplace. Niche markets are forming daily, and the growth of cyberspace has threatened traditional marketing strategies. Many companies are facing major hurdles in sustaining growth while they deal with the severe morale problems of an intimidated, overwhelmed workforce.

As Charles Handy proposes, companies must transform while they are successful, not when they reach the point of decline. It takes courageous leadership to balance the competing demands of short-term success and long-term sustainability. Figure 1–1 is an adaptation of Handy's Sigmoid Curve,[3] which provides a compelling image of how organizations must transform at Point A. When enterprises are on the decline and reach Point B, it is too late. In describing the natural cycle of companies, Handy warns that it is necessary to retain the best of past practices while simultaneously introducing new concepts conducive to a changing future.

For our purposes, I have labeled the curves to show *Quality* and *Reengineering* as the wave of the previous decade and *Innovation* as the

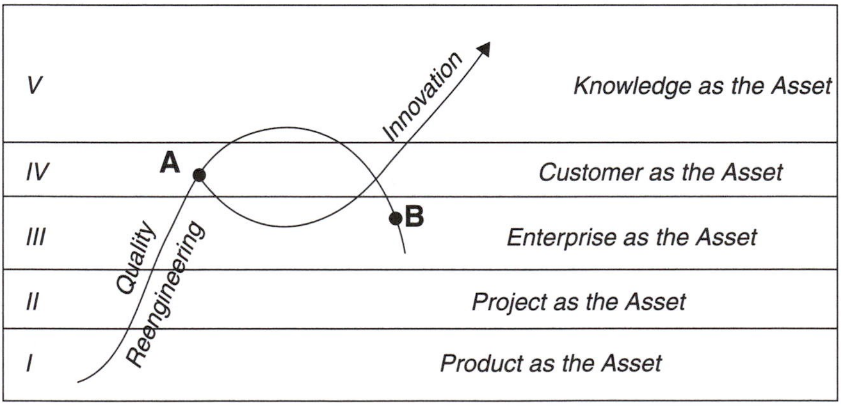

Figure 1–1 Handy's Sigmoid Curve.

wave for the next millennium. This view of the future is not, however, a matter of technological prowess, although technology will continue to play an increasing role in businesses of the future. The evolution of the asset to be managed (i.e., from *technology* to *knowledge*) is outlined in more detail in chapter 2. This is a new concept of innovation defined in terms of intellectual capital, learning, and creativity rather than discrete deliverables. It is a world of transformation rather than technology transfer. It is a world of "innovating" a future rather than focusing on barriers to progress.

As described by Sumantra Ghoshal, an INSEAD professor, and Chris Bartlett, a Harvard professor, today's managers must focus on a new dimension: "the flow of intelligence, ideas and knowledge."[4] This is in addition to the traditional flow of parts, components and finished goods, and/or funds, skills, and other scarce resources. Managers have awakened to the fact that their real responsibility/opportunity is leveraging the intellectual capability of their individual employees and the organization as a whole.

The Case for Knowledge Innovation

In broad terms, the evolution of modern management concepts has been sketched in my article "Knowledge Innovation: The Common Language."[5] At the time, the fall of 1993, it was clear that a concurrent transformation was evolving in all three sectors—education, government, and industry—and that the similarities in mission were beginning to overshadow differences. In 1993, I defined the concept of Knowledge Innovation as "the creation, evolution, exchange and application of new ideas into marketable goods and services for the excellence of an enterprise, the vitality of a nation's economy and the advancement of society as-a-whole."

In chapter 2, these shifts are discussed in more detail, but the three levels outlined below offer a good summary. In some respects, the evolution is natural. What is of most significance is the velocity with which these changes are occurring.

In Figure 1–2, the evolution is outlined according to the elements of analysis, the relationship with the customer, and the overall management style. *First*, the earlier years of the computer industry were data-intensive; there was a focus on automation. It is widely recognized that an information economy was spawned with the rapid technological advances that characterize the latter part of the twentieth century. Theoreticians and practitioners alike now realize that what is

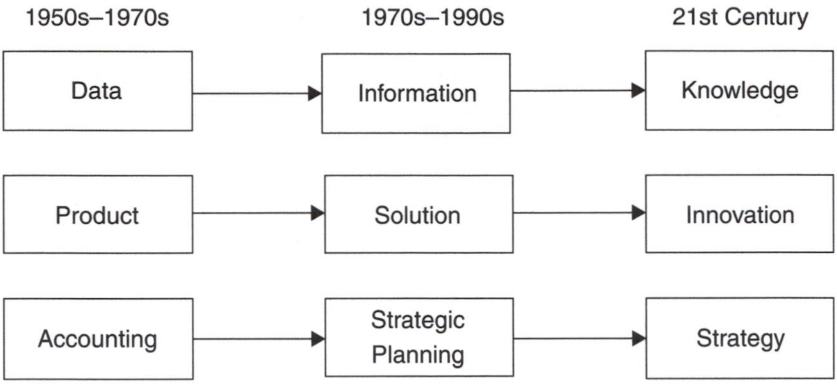

Figure 1–2 Evolution of Thought.

important is not the information per se, but the context in which ideas are used and what value they contribute to the organization. Now, we can understand that knowledge about products and processes may be more valuable than the products themselves.

Second, the primary focus in many industries has been product-oriented: build the best mousetrap and the sales organization need only take orders. By the 1970s, competition intensified and attention shifted toward the customer or the consumer, depending on the industry. Elaborate market segmentation schemes were developed and a packaging of solutions and systems integration became a priority. Modern management will demand a much more integral role with customers, and enterprises will become far more "innovative" in the relationships and partnerships they develop with key clients. This is the ideal way to create, transfer, and apply new knowledge within and across industries.

Third, the focus changed in how organizations are managed. Many corporations and business schools have been criticized for their finance/accounting approaches to management. In the 1970s, the strategic planning profession emerged with statistical tracking mechanisms and comprehensive planning processes and tools. Given the dynamics of the current marketplace, corporate planning has become much more a matter of strategy and the art of leadership than of sophisticated plans.

There has been a (re)birth of the principles and practices related to education, development, and learning. With the advancement of technology and the increasing complexities of the marketplace, executives began to realize that learning no longer could be isolated to the classroom. A new *community of practice* emerged to focus on the learning organization. Ray Stata, Chairman and CEO of Analog Devices, in a *Sloan Management Review* article described the business implications: "an organization's capacity to learn as their only sustainable competitive advantage—especially in knowledge-intensive industries."[6] An entire new way to view the innovation process was born.

One way to show the relationship between these key elements of modern management is presented in Figure 1–3.

Managers need to focus on *knowledge* as the evolution from data and information. This provides a way to describe the *content* that needs to be managed. The second focus is on *innovation* as the *process.* However, in this regard we are framing the process from the movement of ideas rather than the advance of technology per se. The *methodology,* which is the real-time *learning,* is the only way to increase the content level of knowledge and ensure business results through the full innovation process. The increasing spiral represents an accumulation of value throughout the process if both domains (i.e., content and process) are managed simultaneously. Anything less is a suboptimal strategy.

Current market conditions are likely to intensify over the next decade. Organizations must develop new ways to incentivize, capture,

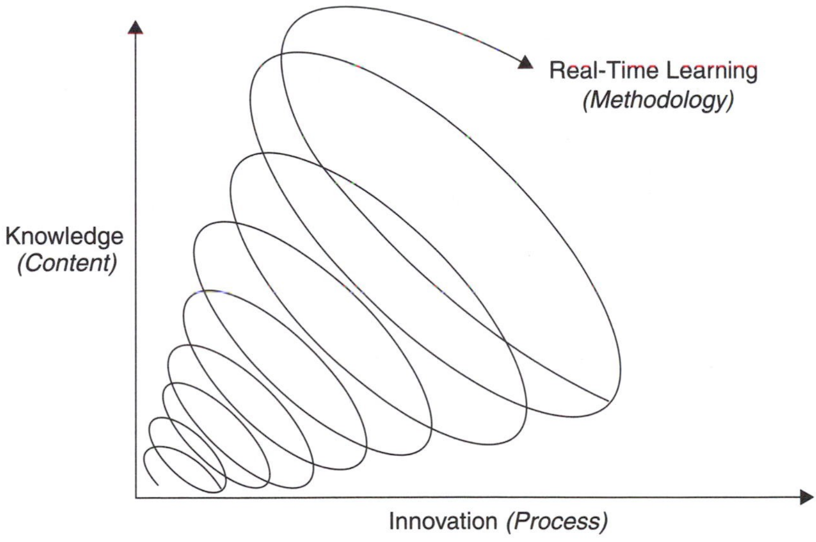

Figure 1–3 Integrated Focus: Knowledge and Innovation.

and utilize new ideas expeditiously. The intangibles must become measurable in both qualitative and quantitative terms. The answers are unlikely to be found in current practices. In fact, the most superior benchmarking capabilities of best practices—even in knowledge management—can provide only signals of direction as companies try to gauge their proximity to the norms of best-in-class. If Handy is right, however, the answers may not be found in what others are doing, but will more likely be discovered with an organization's rededication to its own sense of purpose coupled with flexible management systems that balance the need for quality and creativity simultaneously.

In retrospect, one can see the impact of managerial changes from multiple world perspectives. Asian competition has prompted unparalleled collaborative research initiatives in the United States. The target of a unified European Community by 1992 prompted similar research initiatives in both the "hard" and "soft" sciences. Moreover, we get a sense that the emphasis on cycle time is the worldwide business challenge that requires a receptivity to innovation never before demanded. Given that these changes are fundamental and pervade every dimension of the management system, it is clear why innovation management cannot be left to serendipity.

When one analyzes the concepts of cycle time and of idea-to-market, the full spectrum of activity comes into play. Few organizations, however, have made the innovation process explicit. For years, the domain of innovation strategy belonged to the R&D professionals—and still does when viewed from a technological perspective. However, modern managerial practice respects that good ideas can—and must—come from everywhere in the enterprise and should have the opportunity to flourish and be converted into marketable products and services. The true value-added contribution of individuals is proportionate to their capability to learn and ability to apply their learnings real-time whatever their managerial level, whatever the task, whenever the opportunity presents itself.

The Momentum of Knowledge Management

What began almost ten years ago—Knowledge Innovation™*—has now reached the stage of a critical mass of insight. Dedicated profes-

---

* Knowledge Innovation™ is a trademark of Entovation International. All rights reserved.

sionals across all disciplines are exploring and defining new management practices fundamental to capitalizing on the knowledge-based economy. Although there has been a plethora of articles and books on the topic, the seminal cookbook (if there ever can be such a thing) is only "work in process." In the 1950s, when Alfred P. Sloan divisionalized General Motors, it sent a clear, consistent, concise message about the techniques necessary for large-scale business management. However, today, driven by the acceleration of computer/communications technology and the value of collaborative networks, the real competitive differentiator—human talent—provides the enterprise advantage.

Today, the emerging community of practice transcends any function, sector, industry, or geography. Participants include theorists and practitioners from education/learning systems, economics/finance, quality/benchmarking, human resources, information/Internet technology, R&D/innovation strategy, and more. The concurrent engineering, agile manufacturing, and reengineering initiatives are all coming to a common theme: transformation of the enterprise—profit or not-for-profit—through knowledge management. Collective findings are emerging:

1. The knowledge movement is pervasive. Whether it is defined in terms of learning, intellectual capital, knowledge assets, intelligence, know-how, insight, or wisdom, the conclusion is the same: manage it better or perish. Initiatives in industry, education, and government are trying to tackle the same problems, issues, and opportunities.

2. The unmeasurable must be measured. If it cannot be measured, it isn't considered of value. However, traditional financial accounting mechanisms fail to calculate/calibrate the most important resource of the firm: its intellectual capacity. Instead, current mechanisms treat people as liabilities or expenses instead of assets. The business case must be defined in order to justify necessary investment strategies in the human and social (i.e., interactive) capital of the firm.

3. A collaborative research base must be established. There is minimal research activity for service functions or the services industry of the economy. There is no equivalent to the Industrial Research Institute for the services industry—the fastest-growing sector of the economy. There is minimal government funding and few consortia that are non-industrial in mission. Enterprises are embarking on individual R&D efforts when a collective degree of research—on a precompetitive basis—is essential for establishing a solid foundation for the future of the industry.

4. Initiatives must be designed as "middle-up-down." Top-down leadership continues to be essential for management because traditional hierarchical structures will not disappear overnight. Grassroots activities that are networked can provide the insight for change validated by those closest to the point-of-sale. Oftentimes, those closest to service delivery are not the people empowered in an organization. Hubert Saint-Onge, CIBC, describes the strategy as middle-up-down as a way to balance and integrate the best of both methods.

5. Insight is being gleaned rapidly. For those who embrace change as reality, there is little time to be spent on barriers. The future is far more exciting to create. In each profession, those who have been deemed philosophers and futurists are being sought for counsel on business operations. What was theory yesterday is fundamental to business survival tomorrow. There is a cumulative effect between and among disciplines as leaders seek to understand the principles and policies of one another. Indeed, the field has become sufficiently sophisticated to warrant the benchmarking of best practices for even further dissemination and leverage.

6. Implementation takes many forms. New titles and program initiatives vary from company to company due to the uniqueness of each corporate culture. New titles range from novel verbiage to relabeling of traditional functions. There are many ways to (re)configure the knowledge puzzle, and leadership can come from any level, function, or position in the company.

7. Management architectures are useful, but should not be limiting. A frame of reference is essential in order to scrutinize and interconnect the variables. However, exploration of the known factors leads to identification of new variables and interconnections that are fundamental to the business. The frame provides a way to organize the discussion and fuse the diverse values within the company culture. The process must be dynamic—not static—in order to capitalize on new business opportunities coming from unserved markets and unarticulated needs.

8. The nature of "the collective" must be understood and engaged. Enterprises are now defined as including multiple stakeholders: suppliers, partners, alliances, customers, and—in some cases—competitors. These infrastructures are a combination of evolving, ecological systems and carefully architected schemes for profitable growth. The combination is what is of most value. Attention must now focus on the definition of the whole and the symbiosis of the pieces.

9. Technology is integral to the successful functioning of the knowledge enterprise, but how? Similar to the misconceptions of computer-based education, artificial intelligence, and the early renditions of groupware, there is confusion as to the appropriate role for the supporting technology. The "productivity paradox" explains why there has not been a commensurate economic return for the investment in technology (i.e., behavioral disconnects), but it does not provide a path forward for the ideal technical solutions. This will take some time and considerable trial and error.

10. The knowledge phenomenon must be managed and not left to serendipity. As incomplete as the systems may be, some influence and control is better than none at all. Consider the kaleidoscope, which when moved in small degrees changes the image; but there are the inevitable unexpected forces that cause a major shift in orientation. Management must be understood as both a science and an art in order to reap optimal advantage.

The interest generated over the past year is significant. Business schools have created interdisciplinary initiatives by necessity. Industrial investments have forged connections that were not likely to occur otherwise. Government agencies are also, by necessity, forced to produce significantly more results to the consumer than can be provided with incremental improvements. Reengineering and quality efforts—along with massive restructuring—have reaped what financial results are possible. Realignments are now needed in order to fulfill expectations of stakeholders.

The paradigm will shift. It is inevitable. This focus on knowledge as the foundation for a successful future has been embraced. Creativity is being reborn in ways to contribute to the bottom line of an enterprise. As impure as this new science may be, it provides insights not easily discerned with traditional management methodologies. Experimentation is rampant, and people seek to learn from their mistakes as well as the successes and failures of others.

Summary

Out of the depths of a painful restructuring process comes an understanding of fundamental new variables that cannot be left to serendipity. There is a new appreciation for the human dimension of the organization and the value of intellectual capital. Managers have discovered the need for a creativity and growth equation to match the rigor of productivity investments. Furthermore, there is a realization that change must be embraced rather than feared. It must be seen as the foundation for progress. There is more leverage in *innovating* a future than in creating plans only as incremental extrapolations of the past. Indeed, a new consciousness is emerging, one that is based on trust, mutual respect, and the value of diversity in every dimension.

The basic premise of this book is that moving theory to practice—the process of *innovation*—expeditiously is the ultimate managerial challenge of the next decade and beyond. It is at the heart of business survival, transformation, and eventual sustainability. This applies if you are an academic practitioner, an industrial manager, or a government official. It affects those in the services sector as much as the manufacturing sector. It must be integral to your strategy whether you represent an industrialized nation or a developing country. Only with a fundamental understanding of the innovation process and how it evolves in your own work environment can you develop distinct competencies that will make you and your organization competitive and viable in the future.

The knowledge movement is reshaping the very foundation of how an organization is created, evolves, matures, dies, or is reformed. The shifts are fundamental in reshaping the way we do business, how economies are developed, and how societies prosper.

Notes

1. Roshi Philip Kapleau, *The Three Pillars of Zen: 25th Anniversary Edition* (New York: Doubleday Dell Publishing, 1980).
2. Debra M. Amidon Rogers, *Global Innovation Strategy: Creating Value-Added Alliances* (Austin, TX: IC^2, University of Texas, 1989).
3. Charles Handy, *The Age of Paradox* (Boston: Harvard Business School Press, 1989).
4. Christopher A. Bartlett and Sumantra Ghoshal, "Managing Across Borders: New Strategic Response," *Sloan Management Review* (Fall 1987).
5. Debra M. Amidon Rogers, "Knowledge Innovation: The Common Language," *Journal of Technology Studies* (Fall 1993).
6. Ray Stata, "Organizational Learning—The Key to Management Innovation," *Sloan Management Review* (Spring 1989): 64.

2

Kaleidoscopic Dynamics

In the memory of man, no invention, and no work,
whether addressed to the imagination or to the understanding,
ever produced such an effect.
A universal mania for the instrument seized all classes,
from the lowest to the highest,
from the most ignorant to the most learned,
and every person not only felt, but expressed the feeling
that a new pleasure had been added to their existence.

KALEIDOSCOPE RENAISSANCE[1]

Imagine for a moment that you are peering through a kaleidoscope, one with many vibrant colors of glass, elaborate pearls, and a variety of precious metals—silver, gold, and copper. As you turn the barrel, the image changes shape...a little. You turn the barrel again the same amount, and the image changes again...a little. Then you touch it ever so slightly and the entire image takes a new form. For some reason, the combination of the slight movement and the natural laws of physics has changed the reflection...forever. At that moment, you realize that you cannot return to the previous image and you must move forward.

Similarly, enterprises have undergone unprecedented change. Some adjustments have been by design; the remainder have naturally evolved. Each has had an impact on the other. Some adjustments—however carefully constructed—have not produced anticipated results. In many instances, the reverse effects may have occurred. Then, there are those times when the unexpected just happens and you cannot seem to trace the roots of a successful venture. It is a breakthrough of sorts—the effect of a multiplicity of factors coming together and producing a certain result. It can come in the form of a research discovery that so catapults the application possibilities that even current research seems obsolete. It can be in the form of a market acceptance that demands more of the technology than product engineers ever imagined. It can come in the form of a managerial set of experiences during which the collective insights of a team produce something far beyond what any combination of individuals might otherwise have created. Once experienced, there is no turning back. The only alternative is to continue to move toward a redefined vision, the path of which may be architected, but, for the most part, is subjected to that unknown combination of forces.

How does one manage in an environment subject to so many interdependent variables—known and unknown? In some respects, effective leaders seem to revel in the wonder of it all, control what they can, and leave the rest to human and mother nature. This is the essence of a dynamic global economy in constant motion, shaping and being reshaped by daily and strategic decision-making at every economic level. As described by Margaret Wheatley in *Leadership and the New Science,* amid the apparent chaos there is a natural order of things. Patterns emerge from which we can discern the next steps forward. She speaks of "the constant weaving of relationships...energies that merge and change...a ballet of chaos and order, of change and stability, as two complementary aspects in the process of growth."[2]

Fundamental Managerial Trends

Our top leadership has evolved from a past in which command and control was the managerial order of the day. Many are trying to manage organizations in dynamic business environments with fifty-year-old management technology. The more progressive concepts may seem quite foreign and very difficult to justify. How does one create a rationale and a business plan for an unserved market and unarticulated needs? The fundamental market changes of uncertainty have transformed the core role of executive leadership into one of trust, learning, and inspired vision.

Historically, good managers were able to create a high-quality product or family of products, identify the potential market, develop a strategy, and leverage off results. The current kaleidoscopic environment prohibits such simple, linear successes. Amid dramatic change, organizations must create ways to "manage stability and change" simultaneously, according to the management philosopher Henry Mintzberg.[3]

We live in an interdependent world. Independence is no longer a viable managerial option. Similarly, changes do not occur in a vacuum. One change has an automatic effect on another series of variables, and, subsequently, they are affected by those changes—usually in unexpected ways.

In a paper entitled "The Challenge of 5th Generation R&D: Virtual Learning," I defined the evolution of modern management.[4] The reality is that there are hundreds—maybe thousands—of key variables that are integral to the survival of an enterprise. There are at least five major forces influencing the worldwide marketplace that must be understood in order to capitalize on the business opportunities afforded by the global economy:

Shift from Information to Knowledge

In the information technology profession, there has been a natural evolution of computing. *Data* are elements of analysis. *Information* is data with context. *Knowledge* is information with meaning. *Wisdom* is knowledge plus insight. When applied to any community, these concepts refer to the sum total experience and learning residing within an individual, group, enterprise, or nation. The new source of wealth is knowledge, not labor, land, or financial capital. It is the intangible, intellectual assets that must be managed.

The shift in orientation from information to knowledge is not a cosmetic change. It requires an entirely new lens through which the world is viewed. From this moment on, we understand the human dynamics of the organization and the importance of the human element. But what is it about people that is important? What constitutes value-added? The answer, naturally, is the *knowledge* they have to contribute to the business and their innate capability to continue to do so. Moreover, it is the ability of groups to learn from one another and contribute collectively to the solution of a problem and/or the identification of a new business opportunity.

Professionals have found themselves on "information overload" and starved for knowledge—the downside of a technologically sophisticated society. The challenge, then, is to develop mechanisms to ensure that time—the most precious commodity of all—is spent on genuine value-added activities. More important, mechanisms need to be established to be able to project viable businesses in the future when our current practices track trends.

Shift from Bureaucracies to Networks

The traditional hierarchical designs that served the industrial era are not flexible enough to harness the full intellectual capability of an organization. Much more less constrained, fluid, networked organization forms are needed for effective modern decision-making. The *Strategic Business Units* (SBUs) of the Alfred P. Sloan era have given way to the creation and effective utilization of *Strategic Business Networks* (SBNs) however they may be defined by a given enterprise. Progressive organizations establish *Strategic Business Systems* (SBS's) with multiple networks, interdependent units, and dual communications.

Another new lens from which the organization must be viewed is the shift from hierarchical authority to a system based on new ideas—and the performance thereof. A marketplace reliant on the flow of new ideas cannot restrict from where those ideas originate. By definition, boundaries are shattered. Organizations seek valuable contributions both inside and external to the firm. The *Strategic Business Network* (SBN) now includes partners, suppliers, and other stakeholders, including customers and sometimes competitors.

Reality is that effective organizations are neither hierarchical nor networked, but a blend of both. This is the true cultural challenge. Based on a company's traditions and values, different priorities would be placed on the management spectrum. The important thing is that there is a flexibility built into the managerial system to capitalize on opportunities while at the same time ensure proper responsibility and accountability. This notion of "constrained freedom" is far more complex than it appears.

Shift from Training/Development to Learning

The role of education has become paramount in all organizations—public and private. However, the change has been from a passive orientation with a focus on the trainer and the curriculum to an active perspective that places the learner at the heart of the activity. In fact, learning must occur real-time in both structured and informal ways. Detailed curriculums have given way to action research by teams as the best way to advance the knowledge base.

The new lens requires you to realize the real-time value of learning—in the classroom...on the job...in all customer and professional interactions. Learning is *the* integral process for progress. It is an investment rather than perceived expense to the organization. The knowledge that one creates and applies is more important than the knowledge one accumulates. New techniques, such as collaborative teams and action research, can be incorporated easily into the culture.

The tragedy of current educational practices is that they are intended to create a learning ability (i.e., the capacity to create new ideas). Indeed, new ideas are usually generated through the process; but there are no institutionalized mechanisms to capture those ideas, nurture them, and create new products and processes. They tend to be lost in the system. Most evaluation systems measure the "quality" of the training instruments rather than assessing the actual value of the process itself.

Shift from Local/National to Transnational

No longer can enterprises rely on purely regional approaches to maintain their profitable growth. More and more, companies and industries of all types are needing to globalize in order to maximize their profits. The fact is that every national strategy must be created within an international context—thus, the term *transnational.* After World War II, there was a need to create mechanisms (e.g., the World Bank and the IMF) to move capital around the world. During this post–Cold War era, there is a need to create the equivalent for "*the world trade of ideas.*"

This is the new lens that may require the most adjustment of all—especially for U.S.–based operations. For most companies experiencing productivity measures, one of the first expenses to be eliminated is international travel at the same time when an understanding of multiple cultures is essential to future global business success. This is the lens that begs a strategy of collaboration versus competition. It is the same lens that demands a view of the whole in order to understand the interrelationship of the parts.

Acceleration of communications technology has expanded the definition of potential business. Alliances of all forms are necessary in order to enter the playing field. There is no way that an organization can easily survive without an integral relationship with partners, suppliers, and other stockholders. Cultural differences must disappear and leveraging distinctive competencies is the only recipe for survival.

Shift from Competitive to Collaborative Strategy

We live in an era of competitive strategy—one that produces only win/lose scenarios. Even in a cooperative environment, parties divide up the wealth to create a win/win. The pie, however, remains the same. With a collaborative approach, symbiosis creates a larger pie to share or more pies to divide. Alliances of every dimension are the natural order of the day in realization that go-it-alone strategies are almost always suboptimal.

The last decade has been bursting with institutionalized examples of competitive strategy. Shakespeare once wrote: "He drew a circle to shut me out...heretic, rebel, a thing to flout; But love and I had the wit to win, we drew a circle that took him in." It is time to remove the barriers to progress and to establish mechanisms of communication and partnership that transcend current practice.

Trust is a very precious value. With the emergence of an interdependent, global economy, such faith is essential. Beyond the obvious advantages of shared resources is an understanding that there must be a more effective way to increase the standard of living of all of our countries simultaneously. This is our collective agenda...nothing less.

The shifts just outlined are monumental in scope. They influence every aspect of the business from ideas for new products/services to the resultant impact in the marketplace. They cannot be overlooked. The dynamic effect, however, is that each major shift is having a compounding impact on the others. The end result is continued uncertainty about what the future may hold.

There are numerous other fundamental changes, but for the purpose of understanding the integral role of knowledge in innovation management, these will suffice. The assumption is that these shifts—and other attempts to balance the traditional with the new—are fundamental and permanent. There is no turning the kaleidoscope back to a previous image. Understanding the implications for managing your organization forward will be essential to your personal career and organization's success.

Fifth-Generation Enterprises

In 1990, Charles Savage published *Fifth Generation Management,* which was named the best management book of the year by Tom Peters.[5] Savage outlined a new set of management principles: peer-to-peer networking, integrative processes, work as dialogue, human time and timing, and virtual task-focusing teams. He described the "invisible networks"—which have come to be known as "communities of practice"—as constituting the real strength of a company.

We now have some perspective on this rapidly unfolding modern management philosophy—from where it has come and where it may lead. In Figure 2–1 (previously published in *Research-Technology Management*), the evolution is mapped according to the primary asset to be managed: technology/product, project, enterprise, customer, and knowledge. Although it is difficult to make such gross generalizations, it is instructive to have a sense of contrast in the elements based on the management architecture that will be detailed in chapter 6: performance, structure, people, process, and technology. It also shows the succession of customer focus from retention to satisfaction and, ultimately, to success—concepts that are defined in more detail in chapter 9.

Primary data for the first three generations was derived from *Third Generation R&D: Managing the Link to Corporate Strategy,* written by three Arthur D. Little senior executive consultants.[6] By contrasting organizations, they were able to identify some distinctions in operating philosophy and resource allocation decisions. Dr. William A. Miller, vice president for research and business development, Steelcase North America, has outlined how customers must be integral to the R&D process and the sustainability of the business as a whole. His findings provide the foundation for the fourth generation.[7] The fifth

	1st Product as the Asset	*2nd Project as the Asset*	*3rd Enterprise as the Asset*	*4th Customer as the Asset*	*5th Knowledge as the Asset*
Core Strategy	• Function in Isolation	• Link to Business	• Technology/ Business Integration	• Integration With Customer R&D	• Collaborative Innovation System
Change Factors	• Unpredictable Serendipity	• Inter-dependence	• Systematic Management	• Accelerated Discontinuous Global Change	• Kaleidoscopic Dynamics
Performance	• Function as Overhead	• Cost Sharing	• Balancing Risk/Reward	• "Productivity Paradox"	• Intellectual Capacity/ Impact
Structure	• Hierarchical; Functionally Driven	• Matrix	• Distributed Coordination	• Multidimensional "Communities of Practice"	• Symbiotic Networks
People	• We/They Competition	• Proactive Cooperation	• Structured Collaboration	• Focus on Values and Capability	• Self-Managing Knowledge Workers
Process	• Minimal Communication	• Project-to-Project Basis	• Purposeful R&D/Portfolio	• Feedback Loops and "information persistence"	• Cross-Boundary Learning and Knowledge Flow
Technology	• Embryonic	• Data-Based	• Information-Based	• IT as a Competitive Weapon	• Intelligent Knowledge Processors
	Customer *Retention* →		Customer *Satisfaction* →		Customer *Success* →

Management Operations (Performance through Technology)

Figure 2–1 Contrast in Business Generations. *(Source: Debra M. Amidon Rogers, "The Challenge of 5th Generation R&D: Virtual Learning,"* Research-Technology Management *[July–August 1996]: 36.)*

generation—recognizing *knowledge* as the asset to be managed—has been compiled from the collective insight contained in the books and trends referenced, as well as interaction with what I call lead *ken* practitioners.

> *First-Generation Business.* Functions tend to operate in isolation with decision-making processes left to serendipity and with unpredictable results. Functions are perceived as overhead and are hierarchically driven. Communication across functions is limited due to the we/they competitive activities—especially through the budget allocation process. Information technology is limited to a select few, and investments are made within groups or divisions. The asset to be managed is the *technology* or the *product/service* specific to the particular industry.
>
> *Second-Generation Business.* Functions begin to link with select business organizations. There is a realization that factors known by others may be needed for successful product development. This increased interdependence and new focus on the market fosters cooperation and communication across functions and business units. Management strategies include cost-sharing matrices, and resource decisions are made on a project-to-project basis within defined funding parameters. Technology support systems are primarily data-based with emphasis on statistical analysis and synthesis. The *project* is the asset to be managed. In both the first and second generation, the focus is on *customer retention.*
>
> *Third-Generation Business.* Functional leaders begin to reach across the entire enterprise, creating formal linkages with business units as a way to manage technology/business integration. Management becomes more systematic through a joint exploration of business portfolio decisions. This management style provides for a more holistic view of the organization with structured collaboration in the name of purposeful R&D investment decisions. Supporting computer technology is more information-based in recognition of the value of the context of the data. The *enterprise* is the asset to be managed, and *customer satisfaction* is a primary quality target.
>
> *Fourth-Generation Business.* All functional and business unit managers realize that a concurrent learning process in consort with customers is the only way to deal effectively with the accelerated pace and global scale of change. Enterprises, now experimenting with information technology as a competitive weapon, are forced

to address the "productivity paradox," by which capital investments in technology do not yield commensurate improvements in business results.

Risk must be balanced with the business opportunity factor, which decreases over time. In building capabilities—individual and group—to meet market needs, new ideas must be validated in practice. Eventually, the new capabilities lead to viable products and services and potentially new businesses all together. Cross-disciplinary insight being essential, "communities of practice" emerge, which are integral to understanding future business opportunities. *Customer* is the asset to be managed, and a new relationship with the customer emerges.

Fifth-Generation Business. Management practices to bring enterprises into the next millennium must be knowledge-based. Systems must be collaborative—not competitive or even cooperative—and the focus on the entire innovation system must include suppliers, distributors, and other stakeholders, including customers and even competitors. Such Strategic Business Systems (SBS's) operate amid kaleidoscopic change, the dynamics of which will accelerate over time.

Business performance will be measured in terms of intellectual assets and the ability to create and apply new ideas in a volatile marketplace. Symbiotic learning networks—electronic and human—are as essential to day-to-day operations as they are to business strategy formulation.

All participants in the innovation system are self-motivating and responsible for creating new knowledge as a way of contributing value to the corporation and customers. Managers will monitor the "flow of knowledge" with the same rigor as they previously managed the flow of capital, parts, and materials. Information technology, with sophisticated computer and communications systems, will embody knowledge-processing capabilities that learn and feed forward intelligence to all participants throughout the enterprise. *Knowledge* is the asset to be managed, and a new focus on *customer success* provides a progressive way to together create a future.

No organization will fit entirely under one category versus another. In fact, if you were to take the matrix above and plot your own organization, chances are that you might discover that you are more advanced in terms of how you manage enterprise-wide processes, but are still using outdated financial performance metrics representative of a first-generation enterprise. On the other hand, you might discover that your organization enjoys an integral partnering relationship with customers, but does not practice the internal cross-boundary learning principles essential to modern management.

Regardless of your findings, it is the discovery process itself that is important. By contrasting your current state with what you believe to be fundamental to your sustainability, management initiatives can be put into place—systematically—so as to optimize your ultimate business performance.

Summary

Change is anything but predictable. Every dimension of the management enterprise has been transforming—moving toward an integration of performance measures, behavioral outcomes, and technology to support collaboration required in twenty-first-century management. No longer can changes be viewed exclusively. It is the compounding effect—similar to the completely new images that appear in a kaleidoscope—that must be taken into consideration as an organization charts its new direction. Once these forces are understood and embraced, they can become linchpins for the process rather than hindrances to success.

Alfred P. Sloan created the management concepts of independence and strategic business units almost fifty years ago. The kaleidoscopic dynamics of today's international networked economy demand new interdependent management technologies (i.e., philosophy, tools, and practices) that are grounded in the principles of idea creation and application—the innovation process.

Notes

1. Cozy Baker, *Kaleidoscope Renaissance* (Annapolis, MD: Beechcliff Books, 1993), pp. 11-12.
2. Margaret J. Wheatley, *Leadership and the New Science: Learning about Organization from an Orderly Universe* (San Francisco: Berrett-Koehler Publishers, 1992), pp. 20-21.
3. Henry Mintzberg, *The Rise and Fall of Strategic Planning* (New York: The Free Press, 1994).
4. Debra M. Amidon Rogers, "The Challenge of 5th Generation R&D: Virtual Learning," *Research-Technology Management* (Washington, DC: Industrial Research Institute, July 1996): pp. 33-34.

5. Charles M. Savage, *Fifth Generation Management: Integrating Enterprises through Human Networking* (Bedford, MA: Digital Press, 1990).
6. Philip A. Roussel, Kamal N. Saad, and Tamara J. Erickson, *Third Generation R&D: Managing the Link to Corporate Strategy* (Boston, MA: Harvard Business School Press, 1991).
7. William A. Miller, "A Broader Mission for R&D," *Research-Technology Management* (November-December 1995): pp. 24-36.

3

Wellsprings Timelines

We live in an age of interdependence
as well as independence—
an age of internationalism as well as nationalism....
The future of the West lies in an Atlantic partnership—
a system of cooperation, interdependence and harmony
where peoples can jointly meet
their burdens and opportunities throughout the world....
Change is the law of life.
And for those who look only to the past or the present
are certain to miss the future.
—*JOHN F. KENNEDY*[1]

The *knowledge innovation* business is complex to say the least. We have all experienced the ups and downs of the past decade with unique paradigms. All of our perspectives are valid; and we need to develop a shared understanding of the past in order to project a better future.

To understand where we are, we must first comprehend where we have been and envision where we would like to go. Each of us has a personal story. We are the products of our upbringing, our education, the people who have influenced us, and the aspirations we hold. To understand the nature of a knowledge economy, we must recognize the power inherent in our expertise and how it might be applied for the good of the whole.

The notion of wellsprings is a powerful metaphor described by Dorothy Leonard-Barton in *Wellsprings of Knowledge: Building and Sustaining the Sources of Innovation*. She claims that "managers of all levels of the organization are the keepers of wellsprings of knowledge. To them falls the responsibility for selecting the correct knowledge sources, for understanding how knowledge is accessed and channeled, and for redirecting flows or fighting contamination."[2] Indeed, the multiple streams of activity have developed a momentum of their own.

What follows is my own account of observations, writings, and events that have influenced my thinking and a possible scenario for catapulting an innovation vision—based on intellectual wealth—forward. Many of the seminal books and articles are referenced throughout this book. The trends I have identified are interwoven in the way I have structured the content and sequence of the chapters. Milestones and conclusions are embedded in the analytic tools offered as a point of reference for your own discovery process. In keeping with the advice of Professors Gary Hamel, London Business School, and C. K. Prahalad, Michigan Business School,[3] I have segmented the material in three timelines: *Hindsight* and *Insight*—summarized below—and *Foresight*, which constitutes my prospectus for the future, outlined in chapter 10.

At this point, I must give due credit (or blame) for the process and results of tracking and projecting my own journey. An Entovation colleague, Francis V. Alla, is the one who insisted that I chart my experiences in some form of a spectrum of activity as a way of determining—for myself—the key influencers in this knowledge movement in which I find myself an active participant. This was not easy. In fact, to say it was painful is to understate the difficulty. On the other hand, what resulted is my own fundamental understanding of a decade of activity and the potential role I might play in converting a vision to reality. After several hours and walls filled with many iterations of flip chart material, I offer a simplified version for you to consider:

1. What is the *timeframe* you would like to scope?
2. List the *references* (e.g., books, articles, videos, etc.) that have shaped your experience during that time period.
3. Determine the key *people* within your sphere of influence (i.e., those who have made an impact on your career and perspective as well as those you may have influenced).

4. Identify the *seminal events* that have played a major role in your given profession(s).
5. Sequence your own professional experience in terms of major *accomplishments*.
6. Draw lines *connecting activities* to indicate their potential interdependency. (Invariably, new events, references, and accomplishments will surface.)
7. Stand back and reflect on *where you've been* and *where you are going*.

This is a project that can be done as an individual, as a team working on a specific project, as an organization at any stage of evolution, or as a *community of practice* with a shared purpose. Treat my own perspective as a way to envision your own direction.

Hindsight

The *Technopolis Strategy* in Japan was built on the history of the original castle towns, according to Sheridan Tatsuno, now president of Dreamscapes, Inc.[4] Similarly, Paul Gray, when retiring from the presidency of MIT, described his role as CEO of the institute as "preserving the best of the past while realigning the rest to be positioned for the future."[5] Indeed, we gain great perspective by understanding the milestones of the past in order to set new goals.

In the emerging field of knowledge management, much progress has been made over the last decade. Figures 3–1 and 3–2 detail the sequence of events, activities, and publications that have formed my perspective of this evolution.

As an educator and government official in education, my own journey based on the acquisition and transmission of knowledge began over thirty years ago. When I entered the corporate arena, however, this focus on knowledge and learning was channeled into a new position titled Strategic Human Resource Planning, where my dual reporting relationship was to personnel and marketing planning. There were no books, no effective management tools, no standards for implementation, not even a common language. And so, our team set about to create the model and process to integrate people planning with business strategy. Similar positions were established in other companies, and a subset of the profession emerged—but what was the profession? The search for ways to manage the value-added contribution of the human

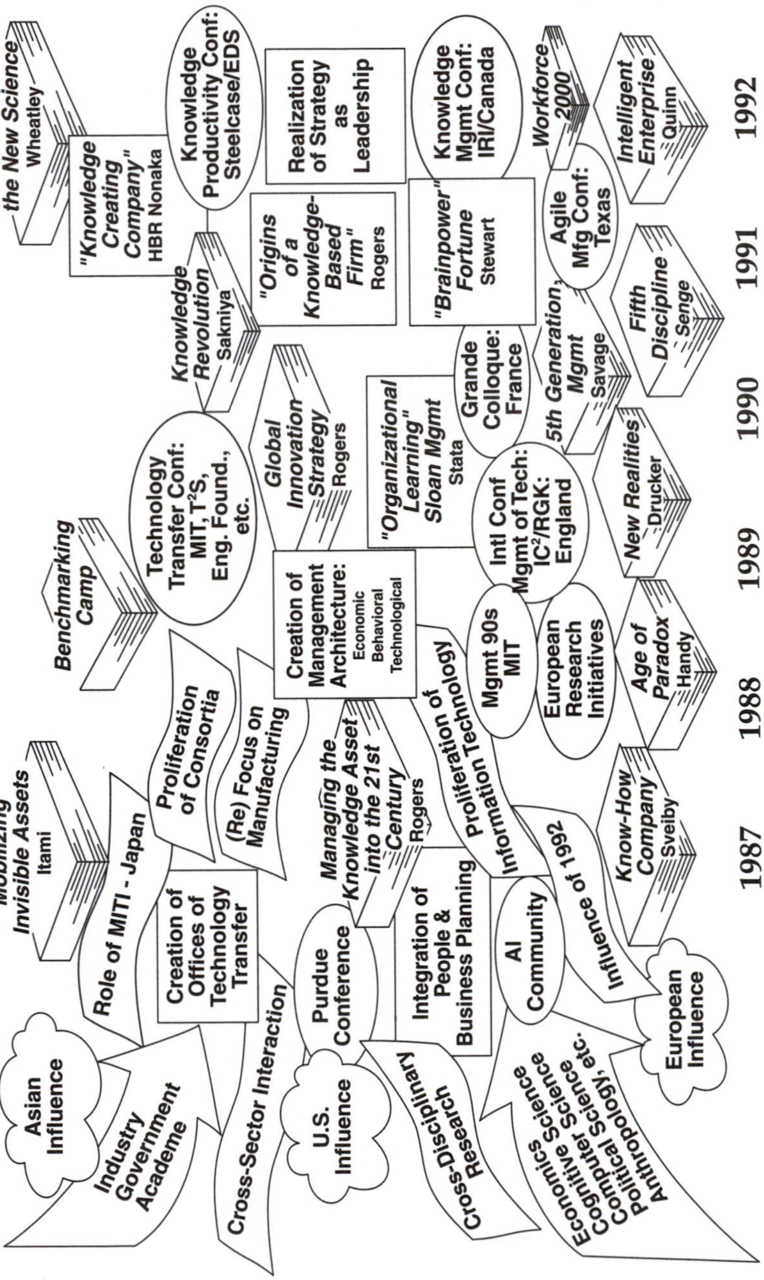

Figure 3–1 Wellsprings Timeline—Hindsight.

element of the business was born, and this search transcended every function.

Subsequently, I assumed responsibility in a newly established function called Planning and Technology Transfer. The world became our "virtual learning laboratory" in which the expertise in academic and government research labs was mainlined into the day-to-day operations of bench engineers.

This organizational structure to augment internal research capacity with external expertise laid the foundation for the focus on knowledge as the asset to be managed, not the technology per se. Many other corporations followed suit, establishing transfer operations in many of the other functions and business units. The network of expertise was created to make investment decisions and manage the process of successfully integrating knowledge gained from research into new products and services.

We had several realizations along the way:

- An idea is a long, long way from a marketable product or service.
- There is significant leverage to be gained from government, industry, and academic interaction.
- The process cannot be left to serendipity.
- Managing across boundaries requires a whole new management philosophy.
- Innovation (i.e., idea to market) cannot be the sole responsibility of the R&D department.
- Knowledge at the source was more valuable than discrete deliverables (e.g., research reports, patents, prototypes, etc.).

By now government agencies in many countries were investing in cross-disciplinary research and sponsoring initiatives to bring together intellectual talent across the sectors (i.e., government, industry, and academe). Spearheaded by the successful role of Japan's Ministry of International Trade and Industry (MITI) in generating mega-research projects and the prosperous practices of Japanese firms in transferring the knowledge embedded in U.S. research activities into their own commercialized products, leaders across the United States and Europe realized the necessity of cooperation if we were to compete successfully in global markets.

The founding of the Microelectronics and Computer Technology Corporation in Austin, Texas, was one visible response that challenged the restrictive "conflict-of-interest" laws. A plethora of research consortia evolved seemingly overnight. Some were government-based; others were industry-sponsored. Some of the most successful provided combinations across the sectors. These consortia afforded participants purpose and time to transcend boundaries that heretofore were rigid demarcations of specialization and isolation. The technology transfer profession dedicated itself to building bridges across different languages, values, and modi operandi.

In Europe, the Japanese challenge was met with a multiyear initiative to unify Europe by the year 1992. That date symbolized the realization that there was value in capitalizing on the economies of scale where there were similarities of purpose and/or resource constraints. The challenge ended up being far more formidable than the architects envisioned, but there is no question that the collaborative activity has made some changes that otherwise never would have happened.

By now, there were many more questions than answers as to how to best manage this new way of working with one another. Legalities and competition aside, there was a need to better comprehend the foundations of communication, learning, and the art of creating new ideas and moving them into the marketplace expeditiously. Our research office had expanded its global presence throughout Europe, Japan, and Australia, and the management challenges became more complex and imperative.

Several research consortia had incorporated technology transfer practices. In 1987, the practitioners were brought together in what has come to be known as a seminal roundtable called "Managing the Knowledge Asset into the 21st Century."[6] Presenters were asked to speak on one of the three stages in the process of innovation—*invention, translation,* and *commercialization*—which had then been defined by Assistant Secretary of Commerce Bruce Merrifield.[7] The realizations were profound, although, at the time, they seemed obvious. In short, the focus needed to be on the entire innovation system in order to compete successfully in the evolving global economy. The challenge was properly stated, but how do we effectively manage such a process rooted in the transfer and leverage of knowledge? A new philosophy of management was forming:

1. **Process:** a concurrent process with numerous feedback loops, not a linear process.
2. **People:** a continuous process of human interactions, not discrete deliverables (e.g., papers, patents, et al.).

3. **Time:** a "real-time" process that occurs at the source, not a sequential process from a to z.
4. **Organization:** requires networked, interdependent collaboration (i.e., not managed hierarchically from the top down).
5. **Push/Pull:** a complementary push/pull process of mediating laboratory capabilities to match market needs, not a push phenomenon of ideas emanating from the lab.

These findings were not isolated in the United States. The same year, Karl Erik Sveiby produced a book entitled *Kunskapsföretaget* (The Know-How Company) in conjunction with a management conference in Sweden.[8] His corporate consulting experience eventually led to the establishment of the first chief officer for Intellectual Capital, Leif Edvinsson, from Skandia, AFS, in 1991. Sveiby identified one severe obstacle: that "there is little or no systematic research and accumulated knowledge on how to manage knowledge-intensive organizations or a service company." We now know that all professions are knowledge-intensive and his identification of the obstacle holds true today.

There were numerous major research initiatives (e.g., ESPRIT, ALVY, etc.) that included in their guidelines an integral relationship with industry to ensure that the knowledge created would eventually result in new products and services to benefit the economy. Many countries hosted study delegations and international conferences to promote the concepts of science research parks and regional economic development activities—initiatives that were proven to be successful in the United States (e.g., Route 128, Silicon Valley). The *Workforce 2000* project crystallized attention on the people aspects of potential business.[9]

We can also trace the Asian influence with a book entitled *Mobilizing the Intangible Assets* published by Hiroyuki Itami in the very same year. He links the measurements of market share to the corporate culture, which he defines as "the attitudes the organization takes as common sense and the types of thought processes and kinds of people it values." He goes on to say that the corporate culture gives each person in the firm a common and distinctive method for transmitting and processing information… [and a] common way of seeing things." It "sets the decision-making pattern and establishes the value-system."[10]

Taichi Sakaiya, in the same time period, wrote *The Knowledge-Value Revolution,* in which he describes the creation of "knowledge-value" as being the "mainspring of economic growth and corporate profits."[11] It was Ikujiro Nonaka, however, who should be credited with articulating the role of knowledge in producing continuous innovation in his seminal *Harvard Business Review* article, "The Knowledge-Creating Company."[12] In describing the company as "a living organism (not a machine)," he places the emphasis on ideals as well as ideas. In his "spiral of knowledge," he illustrates how success is a function of making tacit knowledge (e.g., insights, intuitions, and hunches) available for use by the company as a whole by turning it into explicit knowledge. He describes the need for a "common cognitive ground," which is the concept described in more detail in chapter 4.

With a new dedication to understanding the fundamental management changes, an office for Management Systems Research, under the direction of Dr. Ron Smart, chief management architect for Digital Equipment Corporation, was established to design a management architecture and universal managerial standards with the same technical rigor utilized in technical operations.

Today the notion of managerial architectures is commonplace, but in the mid-1980s the concept was not understood in even the best research universities. Projects were funded at the Massachusetts Institute of Technology, Case Western Reserve University, and the London School of Economics, to mention a few. The resulting architecture is defined in detail in chapter 6 of this book.

Ray Stata, chairman of Analog Devices and co-author of *Global Stakes*[13] and *The Innovators*,[14] in one article published by the *Sloan Management Review*[15] transformed the practice of strategic planning into one of organizational learning. In defining "an organization's capacity to learn as their only sustainable competitive advantage—especially in knowledge-intensive industries," he linked the value of systems thinking to the financial performance of his firm. To this day, he remains a success story of how one CEO—with a respect for the value of collaboration—can inspire vision throughout the company resulting in sustained profitable growth. The company has the bottom-line financial results to prove it.

Shortly thereafter, the Artificial Intelligence community embraced an initiative called the International Management of Knowledge Assets (IMKA). This search for expert systems and tools to manage intelligence evolved into a view of knowledge management processes themselves. Dr. Karl Wiig established the Knowledge Research Institute in Arlington, Texas, and published numerous books, first on expert systems specifically[16] and thereafter with a broader perspective for the knowledge engineering profession.[17]

Numerous other streams of activity were contributing to a new focus on the behavior of an organization, including the proliferation of information technology. With few exceptions, companies were not reaping the expected return on investment for significant capital outlays on technology. This "productivity paradox" is eloquently defined in a National Research Council report entitled *Information Technology in the Service Society.*[18] In the closing chapters, it addresses the role of information technology in corporate decision-making and asserts that "more often than not, management makes the difference."

These findings are consistent with the ones reported by A. Crescenzi in an article for *Information Strategy: The Executive's Journal,* in which he describes that only five of the thiry Fortune 500 companies were successful in having a strategic impact through information technology implementation.[19] "The successful companies had joint organizational-technical efforts involving high-level management champions and focused upon business goals, evolutionary development, selling, training and team effort," Crescenzi wrote. This reinforces the need to integrate the economic, behavioral, and technological factors of the firm.

Another major stream of activity was a rededicated focus on manufacturing—the integral sector of the economy in serious performance trouble. The National Center for Manufacturing Science (NCMS) was founded along with numerous regional-based centers dedicated to bootstrapping the manufacturing capability of the United States. The counterpart of the Semiconductor Research Corporation (SRC) for manufacturing—SEMATECH—was created with catalytic funding from the National Science Foundation. The technology transfer infrastructure was carefully designed to include suppliers from the beginning. This approach provides some of the roots of supply-chain management and a progressive view of how external relationships are integral to the success of the business.

In the manufacturing environment, the adoption of Total Quality Management (TQM) and Quality Function Deployment (QFD) methodologies was becoming prevalent—especially the concept of benchmarking. The real contribution to the field was the comprehensive focus on management processes and a repositioning of the customer as integral to the success of the business. Commitment to the quality mandate connected all levels, functions, and business units of the organization.

At this point, I returned to the Massachusetts Institute of Technology as an Alfred P. Sloan Fellow to see how the concepts of knowledge management might be embodied in the rubric of innovation strategy. My thesis, *Global Innovation Strategy: Creating Value-Added Alliances,* provides a systematic view of joint ventures from the perspective of the United States, Europe, and Japan.[20] More important, the Lotus Innovation Model (described in more detail in chapter 5) created a way to move beyond the traditional value-chain thinking of innovation into a more systems view.

At the same time, Peter F. Drucker, the management guru of our time, wrote extensively about the role of "a society of knowledge-workers" in *The New Realities*.[21] His view was one of collegiality and mobility, a view of employees who were neither exploited nor exploiters, people capable of being dependent and independent at the same time. That was in 1989. Who could have imagined the trauma that was to come, in which radical downsizing would be the order of the day—usually without concern for the intellectual capital needed to sustain the firm in the future. Most of the middle managers with exceptional explicit knowledge were severed from some of the major firms known historically for lifetime employment.

The kaleidoscopic dynamics were unleashed and executive management—of profit and not-for-profit organizations—would never be the same. Strategic plans became obsolete as soon as the ink was dry. Tom Stewart, in another seminal article in *Fortune* magazine, "Brainpower," tried to center us with the notion of the value of the intellect to the corporation[22]; but the downsizing, reengineering fever was well under way. Too many companies had failed to heed the warnings of Charles Handy[23] and his Sigmoid Curve, explaining that it was too late to transform while you were in the slope of decline.

Insightful leaders and organizations, however, took up the challenge to understand the unknown—the true relationship between intellectual capital and the sustained profitability of a firm. In 1992, Steelcase North America, under the direction of Dr. William Miller, vice president of research and business development, coordinated a major conference with EDS, Inc., on Knowledge Productivity.[24] The results of the conference were reported at the annual meeting, in Vancouver, Canada, of the Industrial Research Institute (IRI)—the chief research officers of the Fortune 500 firms. This was one of the first conferences in the States where the details of knowledge creation and application were carefully scrutinized—not from the perspective of artificial intelligence software programs, but from the general view of management of the innovation strategy of firms.

Meanwhile, three more seminal books were published: *Fifth Generation Management* by Dr. Charles Savage,[25] *The Fifth Discipline* by Peter Senge,[26] and *Intelligent Enterprise* by James Brian Quinn.[27] All three made a significant contribution to the field by making prominent new managerial concepts, such as human networking, self-empowerment, systems thinking, team learning, interdependence, shared vision, uncodifiable knowledge, and the power of the intellect.

All this activity seemed to culminate in a new view of strategy—from the tracking of previous trends and detailed financial management—to a more fluid, futuristic view of projecting trends and patterns forward. Margaret Wheatley in *Leadership and the New Science* projected confidence amid the chaos and uncertainty.[28] She articulated the need to reconcile individual autonomy with organizational control at every level of the enterprise. As uncomfortable and intangible as her prescription might feel, she provided a foundation on which to venture forth.

Insight

The year 1992 not only launched significant changes on the European scene, but also witnessed a virtual explosion of activities searching for new ways of working in every sector, every industry, every nation of the world. At least five fundamental streams of activity were occurring simultaneously, interweaving concepts among one another: (1) *New Techniques to Measure Intellectual Assets;* (2) *Commitment to Quality and Reengineering;* (3) *New View of the Management of Innovation;* (4) *Artificial Intelligence as Management*; (5) *The Value of Learning Systems Theory;* and (6) *Utilization of Technology as a Competitive Weapon*. Individually, each of these movements would have had a significant impact on doing business. Together, they launched forces that were to change the nature of management forever.

Figure 3–2 continues to illustrate the chronological relationship between prominent theorists and practitioners as well as seminal events. Interestingly enough, these forces affected the three core aspects of the management architecture: *economic, behavioral*, and *technological*, which is one reason why the concepts seemed to gain a momentum on their own. Executives who had resisted change for years began to welcome new approaches with leadership eagerness. The difficulty was, however, that many of these methods were untested, embryonic in form, and incomplete at best. Wall Street was demanding quick fixes, when what was occurring was more on the magnitude of an earthquake than a tremor.

At that moment, many leaders recognized that they didn't have the answers. Strategies that were successful only a few years earlier were not conducive to the complexity and uncertainty posed by an expanding global economy. In search for answers, bold steps were

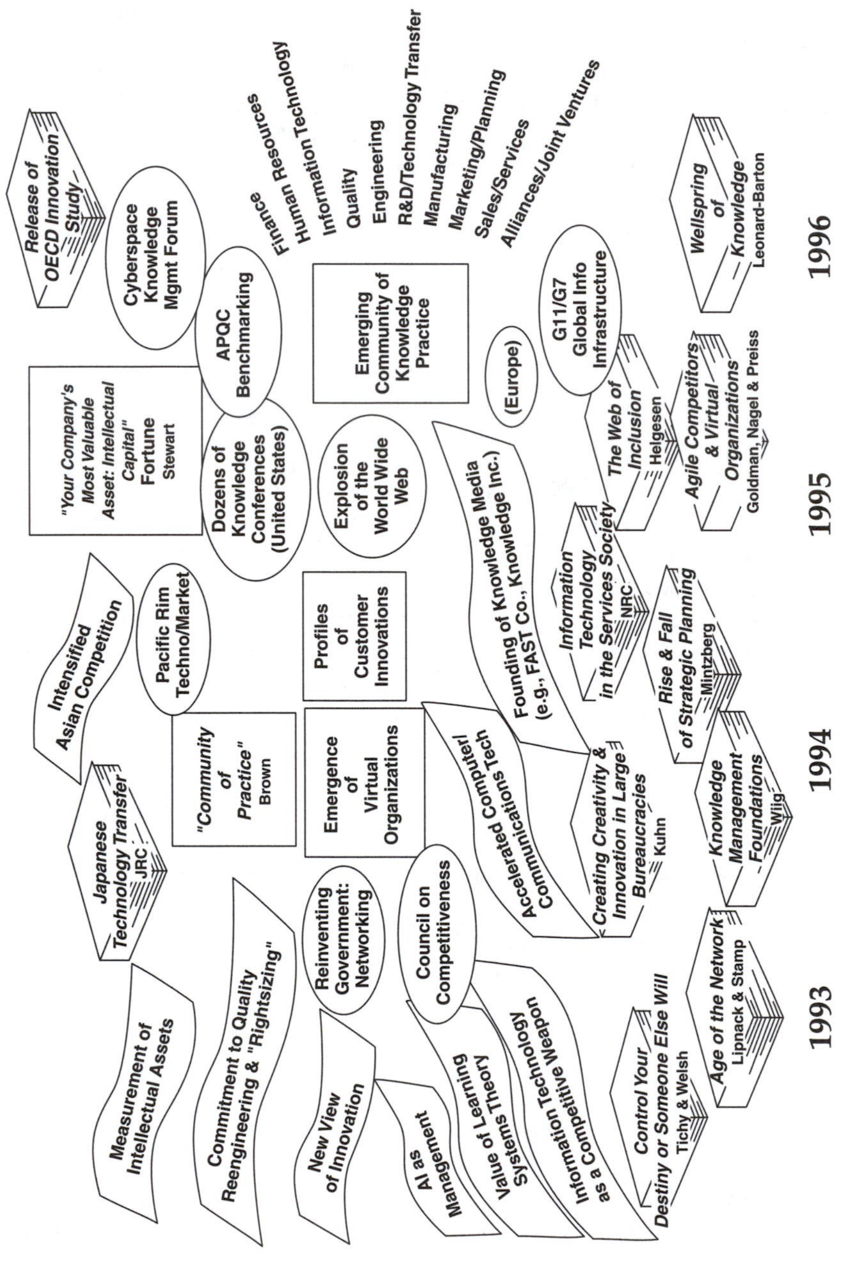

Figure 3–2 Wellsprings Timeline—Insight.

taken and made visible. Jack Welch and Noel Tichy in *Control Your Destiny or Someone Else Will* described the Work-Out program at General Electric, designed to inspire responsibility in every employee of the firm, making them accountable for the success of the company.[29] The Semiconductor Research Corporation, under the leadership of Larry Sumney in 1988, launched the courageous study *Technology Transfer in Japan*, which became a cornerstone document for the GAO international competitiveness report.[30]

With the overwhelming mandate to do more with less, organizations of all types initiated significant cutbacks and downsizing efforts. The U.S. federal government itself, under the leadership of Vice President Al Gore created the "Reinventing Government" initiative and published the principles widely.[31] Successful or not, the process generated an unprecedented number of quality discussions across what previously were considered rigid organizational boundaries. Aided by experts like Jessica Lipnack and Jeffrey Stamps, authors of *The Age of the Network*,[32] government managers were able to realize the power of electronic communications as a way to share ideas, minimize duplication, and infuse creativity into their organizations.

This accelerated acceptance of computer/communications technology promoted the vision of the National Information Infrastructure (NII), which was later relabeled the Global Information Infrastructure (GII) when it was prepared for discussion with the G7. The platform for the NII/GII, which includes provisions for electronic commerce, is defined as "the facilities and services that enable the efficient creation and diffusion of useful information."[33] What is described could, in actuality, be the foundation for an innovation (not information) initiative. In other words, the intent is to establish an infrastructure (e.g., a network) to provide for the optimal flow of useful or meaningful information (i.e., knowledge). This flow of knowledge from creation to application is actually the process of innovation. The resulting outcome is the accelerated creation, movement, and application of new ideas into products and services that benefit society.

The concept of virtual management may be in the process of becoming a discipline in and of itself. Certainly, the modus operandi of networked communication has fueled its research engine in ways we never would have envisioned even a couple of years ago. The National Science and Technology Council (NSTC) of the Office of Science and Technology Policy (OSTP) has nine subcommittees, one of which is dedicated to information science and communications. There are several new research focus areas, one of which is "virtual environments." There is "The Virtual Institute" on the World Wide Web on the Internet, which sponsored the Trinational Institute on Innovation, Competitiveness, and Sustainability. One $1 million ARPA research contract has been dedicated to "Metrics for the Virtual Enterprise." The Agility Forum has an R&D of Agile Virtual Enterprises (AVE) group that is trying to identify organizational, business practice, human, and technology issues. The National Science Foundation has funded a three-year demonstration project for the "Virtual High School of Science and Mathematics," creating a community of scientists, teachers, and learners by using the Internet to deliver a high school curriculum. This represents only a sample of activity likely to accelerate in the generations to come.

This notion of organizational virtuality was best described by John Seely Brown, director of Xerox PARC. In an article published in *FAST Company,* he defines a community of practice that will be discussed in more detail in the next chapter.[34]

The Internet, and in particular the explosion of the World Wide Web with millions of users, has enabled real-time communications, knowledge sharing, and an immediate sense of global presence for both the large and small enterprise. What began as a networking tool for scientific research has become the foundation for day-to-day operations in almost every work environment. Even developing countries are developing leapfrog strategies by mainlining advanced technology into their economic development initiatives. At the same time, free trade practices have become a double-edged sword. On the one hand, one can hardly calibrate the potential business opportunities afforded by the rapidly expanding Asian economy as well as developing nations. At the same time, the intensified international competition demands aggressive but carefully constructed business strategy. Many executives with a not-invented-here (NIH) mentality will have great difficulty adjusting to the new management rules.

In this regard, regions of the world are beginning to address the market as a collective—especially in the Pacific Rim techno-market. Companies and countries are recognizing the power of initially approaching a market together and then competing on their respective uniqueness. Some of this may be due to the realities of geographic constraints and cost of travel, but more likely it is a function of realizing that knowledge is to be gained from interacting with others—even in the same business. Knowledge, unlike labor, land, and financial capital, is a limitless resource and expands when shared or utilized.

Another undercurrent supporting the fast evolution of this movement is the role of the press. Tom Stewart followed up his *Fortune* article on "Brainpower" with another—"Your Company's Most Valuable Asset: Intellectual Capital"—providing an in-depth view of leading practitioners around the world who were assuming the role of Chief Knowledge Officer.[35] In so doing, he began to outline the business opportunity and structured the dialogue among executives across many functions and industries.

Traditionally, it takes months—even years—for new concepts to be published in the academic or business literature. The former co-editors of the *Harvard Business Review,* with the founding of FAST Company, have established a magazine more suited to the dynamic needs of the marketplace. They have developed a knowledge exchange network, a member organization of a select group of companies considered on the leading edge of change. Topics of discussion range from the knowledge revolution itself to the new politics of business.

There is continued evidence of new knowledge media in the form of journals (e.g., *Knowledge/Technology Journal,* published by IC^2 in Austin, Texas), newsletters (e.g., *Knowledge, Inc.,* Mountain View, California), and electronic conferencing (e.g., *Knowledge Management Forum,* West Richland, Washington). Articles now appear in the popular press citing examples of how companies in various corners of the world are beginning to understand the value of managing their intellectual resources rather than leaving them to serendipity.

What began as a few select conferences focused on managing knowledge and know-how in 1989 grew to dozens of conferences sponsored throughout the United States and Europe in the mid-1990s. Almost every consulting firm sponsored a major conference in the fall of 1995 (e.g., Ernst & Young's "The Knowledge Advantage," Arthur Andersen's "Knowledge Imperative," et al.). In fact, most of the firms have developed sophisticated knowledge management practices with management architectures and tools to monitor the learning capacity, the impacts of change management, and/or the flow of knowledge specifically.

On the international scene, conferences are scheduled for Canada, Switzerland, India, Israel, Portugal, and Mexico—to name a few—which will target knowledge management as their theme. In addition, the OECD has released its country-by-country study on innovation[36] and another on literacy, economy, and society,[37] both of which have implications for its new initiative on knowledge. This type of international scrutiny is bound to reinforce the need to shift from an orientation of managing financial capital and the flow of goods to one of valuing the most precious resource of the century—our intellectual assets.

I have focused on one person's journey, my own. Every professional can review the past decade and determine the books, trends, and significant events that have shaped his or her view of the future. (Chapter 10 outlines a prospectus for the future.) From my own perspective, I see an emerging "community of knowledge practice," which will be described in more detail in chapter 4. This virtual network of kindred professionals transcends any function, sector, industry, or geography.

Summary

Hindsight, some say, is the best foresight. You have only to attempt to trace your own influencing factors to realize how complex the world really is. It is only with that understanding of the complexity that you can project a meaningful and relevant future. Each view is valid. We all have our own lenses and are active participants in the theater of innovation.

Remember that the word *ken* is I Ching for "stillness." Only by reflecting—somewhat systematically—can we comprehend our real values and accomplishments and see how they may be applied to our aspirations. There is no other way to confront the challenges afforded by a dynamic global economy and convert apparent crises to opportunities.

Notes

1. Theodore C. Sorensen, *"Let the Word Go Forth"* (New York: Bantam Doubleday Dell Publishing Group, 1988), pp. 322–324.
2. Dorothy Leonard-Barton, *Wellsprings of Knowledge: Building and Sustaining Sources of Innovation* (Boston: Harvard Business School Press, 1995).
3. Gary Hamel and C. K. Prahalad, "Seeing the Future First," *Fortune* (September 1994).
4. Sheridan Tatsuno, *The Technopolis Strategy: Japan, High Technology and the Control of the 21st Century* (Prentice-Hall Press, 1986).
5. Paul Gray, Farewell Address. *MIT Technology Management* (Spring 1989).
6. Debra M. Amidon Rogers and Dan Dimancescu, *Managing the Knowledge Asset into the 21st Century: Focus on Research Consortia* (Cambridge, MA: Technology and Strategy Group, 1987).
7. Bruce Merrifield, "Forces of Change Affecting High Technology Industries." Working document prepared for the U.S. Department of Commerce, 1986.

8. Karl Erik Sveiby and Anders Risling, *Kunskapsföretaget* (The Know-How Company) (Sweden: Liber, 1987).
9. Stuart Margulies, *Workforce Literacy Skills for Jobs 2000* (New York: Educational Design, 1990).
10. Hiroyuki Itami, *Mobilizing Invisible Assets* (Cambridge, MA: Harvard University Press, 1987): p. 23.
11. Taichi Sakaiya, *The Knowledge-Value Revolution* (New York: Kodansha International, 1990).
12. Ikujiro Nonaka, "The Knowledge-Creating Company," *Harvard Business Review* (November-December 1991): 97.
13. James Botkin, Ray Dimancescu, and Ray Stata, *Global Stakes* (New York: Harper & Row, 1982).
14. James Botkin, Ray Dimancescu, and Ray Stata, *The Innovators*. (New York: Harper & Row, 1984).
15. Ray Stata, "Organizational Learning—The Key to Management Innovation," *Sloane Management Review* (Spring 1989).
16. Karl Wiig, *Expert Systems: A Managers Guide* (Geneva, Switzerland: International Labour Office, 1990).
17. Karl Wiig, *Knowledge Management Foundations: Thinking About Thinking* (Arlington, TX: Schema Press, 1993).
18. National Research Council, *Information Technology in the Services Society* (Washington, DC: National Academy Press, 1994), pp. 2–23.
19. A. Crescenzi, "The Dark Side of Strategic IS Implementation," *Information Strategy: The Executive's Journal* 5, no. 1 (1988): 20–29. [Note: cited by Charles C. Holtz in "Organizations and Organizational Support Systems of the Future: Joint Design of Organizations and Computer-Communication-Information Systems," *ThinkWork*, ed. Fred Phillips (Westport, CT: Praeger Press, 1992).]
20. Debra M. Amidon Rogers, *Global Innovation Strategy: Creating Value-Added Alliances* (Austin, TX: IC^2, University of Texas, 1989).
21. Peter F. Drucker, *The New Realities: In Government and Politics, In Economics and Business, In Society and World View* (New York: Harper & Row, 1989), pp. 85, 94.
22. Thomas Stewart, "Brainpower," *Fortune* (June 3, 1991).
23. Charles Handy, *The Age of Paradox* (Boston: Harvard Business School Press, 1989).
24. Lee Bloomquist et al., "Productivity in Knowledge-Intensive Organizations: Integrating the Physical, Social and Informational Environments." Sponsored by Steelcase, EDS, and the Council on Competitiveness (1992).

25. Charles M. Savage, *Fifth Generation Management: Integrating Enterprise through Human Networking* (Bedford, MA: Digital Press, 1990).
26. Peter M. Senge, *The Fifth Discipline: The Art and Practice of the Learning Organization* (New York: Bantam Doubleday Dell Publishing Group, 1990).
27. James Brian Quinn, *The Intelligent Enterprise: A Knowledge and Service Based Paradigm for Industry* (New York: The Free Press, 1992).
28. Margaret J. Wheatley, *Leadership and the New Science* (1992).
29. Noel Tichy and Jack Welch, *Control Your Destiny or Someone Else Will.*
30. Richard Whisnant et al., *SRC Study of Technology Transfer in Japan.* (Research Triangle Park: NC, 1988).
31. Al Gore, *The Gore Report on Reinventing Government: Creating a Government That Works Better and Costs Less* (New York: Times Books, 1993).
32. Jessica Lipnack and Jeffrey Stamps, *The Age of the Network: Organizing Principles for the 21st Century* (Essex Junction, VT: Oliver Wight Publications, 1994).
33. *Putting the Infrastructure to Work* (Washington, DC: U.S. Department of Commerce, 1994).
34. John Seely Brown and Estee Solomon Gray, "After Re-Engineering: The People Are The Company," *FAST Company* (Premier Issue 1995), p. 82.
35. Thomas Stewart, "Your Company's Most Valuable Asset: Intellectual Capital," *Fortune,* October 3, 1994.
36. OECD, *Innovation, Patents and Technological Strategies* (Paris, France: Organization for Economic Co-Operation and Development, 1996).
37. OECD, *Literacy, Economy and Society* (Paris, France: Organization for Economic Co-Operation and Development, 1996).

4

The Emerging "Community of Knowledge Practice"

At the simplest level,
they are a small group of people
who've worked together over a period of time...
not a team, not a task force,
not necessarily an authorized or identified group...
[who] perform the same tasks...
or collaborate on a shared task...
or work together on a product...
They are peers in the execution of "real work."
What holds them together is a common sense of purpose
and a real need to know what the other knows.
—John Seely Brown[1]

At the 1995 International Management Conference of the Strategic Leadership Forum, U.S. Army General Gordon Sullivan described the magnitude of transformation for the military: the need to retain links with the past and simultaneously move into the future. He described the need to perform increasing missions with declining resources and be able to declare a decisive victory at any given moment anywhere in the world. When questioned about the option of supporting a "purple uniform" (i.e., one military force), his response was compelling. "I still believe in diversity," he said, "and the 'complementary competencies' which can be brought to bear on a given situation." With one simple statement, he provided the foundation for the skill convergence needed in a knowledge economy.

John Seely Brown, director of Xerox PARC, and leaders, such as Etienne Wenger, at the Institute for Research on Learning (IRL), a PARC spin-off, have been describing "communities of practice" (defined in the chapter epigraph) for many years. Likely an outgrowth of the quality circles and the evolution of networked learning organizations, this concept can be made explicit as a way to harness the brainpower and creativity of all employees throughout the enterprise. These communities can become centers of expertise that can be highly leveraged in an organization structured to capitalize on economic change and unexpected business opportunities.

After years of research in a variety of industries and on several continents, some modern managerial principles are emerging. It matters not where companies begin (e.g., quality, reengineering, benchmarking, systems thinking, learning networks, restructuring, etc.). There needs to be one compelling force that binds the total organization together, creates that common language and shared purpose. Leadership must come from the top down, the bottom up, and the middle out. In other words, everyone has ownership.

For many organizations, the binding force has been one of change management. No one would argue that the only constant today is the accelerating rate of change. Many CEOs have been successful in mobilizing their organizations to accept and even embrace change as a way of doing business. The way they phrase the challenge is inspiring and people are encouraged—and even rewarded—for doing things differently.

More often than not, however, change management strategies have been met with covert tactics that slow down progress. In some cases, the competition for resources is visible, as is the reduction of risk-taking. In most instances, the damage is more subtle. The communications systems break down. People are not inclined to share their ideas and expertise with others if they feel that their own jobs are in jeopardy. In March 1996, a *New York Times* survey reported that in contrast with the past, 70 percent of workers compete more with co-workers today than they did only a few years ago. Only 20 percent cooperate more.[2] This comes at precisely the same time when collaboration across multiple boundaries is fundamental to business success.

Employees often provide managers what they want to hear, not necessarily the solutions that could provide breakthrough results. When resources are scarce, investments are not made to bring new ideas to the table. In fact, the not-invented-here (NIH) factor is more prevalent at the same time when the marketplace demands a "real-time" incorporation of new ideas.

How do you set in motion the desirable set of processes and practices that will maintain sustainable growth in the uncertain future? The answer is in *innovation strategy,* not change management.

Think for a moment that you are the recipient of these words: YOU must change. You MUST change. You must CHANGE! The normal reaction is one of being in jeopardy. People feel inadequate and resist the degree of change necessary.

Shift gears, and for the moment you are the recipient of these words: YOU must innovate. You MUST innovate. You must INNOVATE! People generally react to these words with a genuine energy for moving forward. They begin to crystallize a vision forward and define how their competencies can be applied to the tasks at hand.

The difference between these two words—*change* and *innovate*—may seem insignificant. However, if you are seeking the binding force to catapult your organization forward, which would you choose? It is the difference between being hit over the head with a hammer or having the wind put at your back. It is the difference between being threatened or inspired.

Convergence of Perspective

What has been observed in the management system as a whole is the transformation of every function and sector of the economy. In some respects, it is the realization that there are *economic, behavioral,* and *technological* dimensions to all the work done in an organization. This broadening of the responsibilities of a function—together with the mandate to develop a collective vision—has established the foundation of a common language and the need for capitalizing on distinctive competencies for competitive advantage.

Over the years, various disciplines or schools of thought have begun to converge on these three interrelated domains. Each, in its own way, is broadening its own scope of theory and integrating core principles from the other domains into its own practice. For instance, *human resource professionals* are seeking to develop more relevant performance measures as well as new ways to use information technology. *Chief information officers,* in order to justify financial investments in technology, are having to better understand the organization structure, motivation of people, and cross-boundary processes. *Quality experts* are probing new ways to facilitate the transfer of knowledge into global best practices. *R&D managers* are taking on new responsibilities for business development in seeking ways to reduce cycle time and develop more integral customer interaction. *Finance professionals* are exploring ways to expand audit capabilities to influence the business strategy of clients and relying on emerging computer and communications technology to do so.

Figure 4–1 shows how professionals in multiple functions across industries and geographies are coming to a common language. If you were to attend a professional meeting of one function or discipline and not know the sponsoring organization, you might be hard pressed to determine the primary focus. The programs—and even many of the presenters—are identical. Each professional orientation is broadening the purview of its responsibilities. There is a realization—and respect for—alternative paradigms that did not exist only a decade ago. Many of these professions appear to have one agenda in common: to understand and optimize the learning capacity of an enterprise to enable a more optimal creation and application of new knowledge (i.e., the process of innovation).

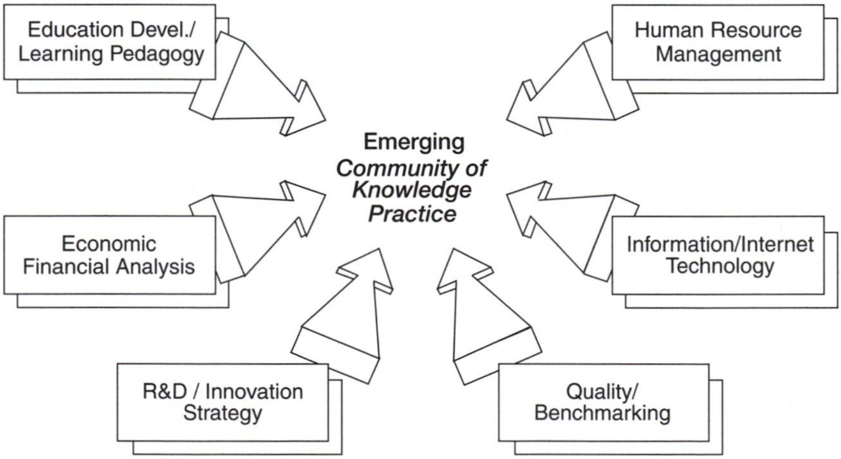

Figure 4–1 Converging Community of "Knowledge Practice."

Simultaneous Transformation

Ken, as a concept, enables us to witness both *perspective* through observation and *perception* of a range of vision at the same time. The traditional view of communities of practice is defined as these evolving learning networks that develop over time and create value-added through a shared mission, but not necessarily a common reporting infrastructure. They may be perceived as professional societies (in fact, new societies and organizations have evolved from them) or they may represent collections of people who transcend any individual discipline, society, or profession.

If the future belongs to those who are able to transform boundaries, then participants in these communities of practice may represent the leadership of tomorrow. Several lead authorities, like *Fortune*'s Tom Stewart and IRL's Etienne Wegner, are in the process of defining what is distinctive about these virtual or invisible networks, while I am observing their commonalties. Regardless of one's perspective, these communities do have a distinct purpose in this evolving knowledge economy. They may be one avenue toward the revitalization of the role of creativity in enterprises, nations, and society as a whole. They provide the counterbalancing force to offset the inevitable negative aspects of quality, reengineering, and downsizing.

The Hopi Indian symbol for homecoming is a spiral in which energy flows from the outside in. If we were to revise the symbol slightly, it would show how energy generated at the center can flow outward. See Figure 4–2. In this regard, we are able to simultaneously scope both the roots and vision of a given segment of the workforce.

There are at least ten functional areas—traditional and new—that are contributing to the emerging community of knowledge practice. In some organizations, there will be fewer; in others, there will be more. New networks are forming daily with the enabling communications technology for intranets and cyberspace. As employees at every level begin to discover that there is more value in creating and applying new ideas than there is in clinging to successes of the past, the numbers and influence of these cross-boundary collections of expertise will increase over time.

For our purpose, we will use a simplified description of mission for the community of knowledge practice: *harnessing complementary competencies with a shared purpose toward a common strategic vision*. Let us take a cursory view of each of these dimensions and the recent changes that characterize their individual evolution. It is the collective changes

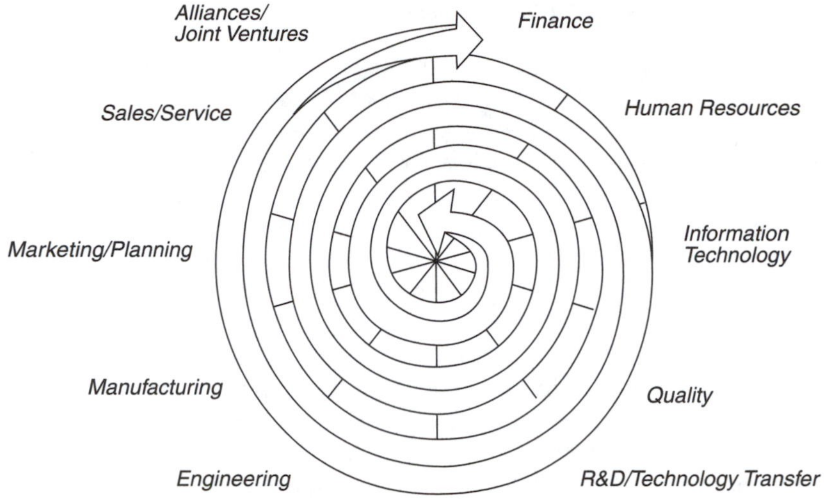

Figure 4–2 Knowledge Communities—Roots and Vision.

that constitute the fundamental transformation under way. Hardly a function, discipline, sector, industry, or organization is unaffected in some significant way.

Finance The name of the game is performance. Whether an organization is profit-based or represents the independent sector, all organizations are struggling with how to deliver more with fewer resources—financial, human, and technical. Modern measures must be systemic and predictive, which implies that previous financial tracking mechanisms may not be enough to monitor sustainable growth in a dynamic interdependent global economy.

The "productivity paradox" is real and a phenomenon that must be addressed. It was originally discovered when companies were not reaping the economic rewards for significant investments in information technology. After careful analysis, it became clear that the problem was behavioral, not technological. In addition, the factors monitored in an expanding economy may not show a desired effect because of the interdependence of the factors themselves. In other words, existing data may not take into account the effect of the intangible assets, such as knowledge capital, social capital, learning capital, and the like.

There has been a major shift from transaction processing to transformation because of the complexity of variables to monitor. Whether one considers the changes in legal/regulatory demands, the degree of mergers/alliances/joint ventures, and/or the broad market and industry restructuring, changing conditions are requiring dramatic changes in policies and practices at every economic level.

The professional response has been one of examining how best to account for the intangible assets on the balance sheet. The Canadian Institute of Chartered Accountants appears to have taken the lead with its 1996 report.[3] But, other countries and regions of the world are following suit. In short, the challenge has become one of accounting for the flow of ideas, knowledge management, and innovation practices.

Human Resources For years there has been an increasing movement to integrate the human resource function into the business. Personnel professionals have sought to become business partners integrated with the bottom-line performance of the company. They have been advocates for investment in the human dimensions of the business in terms of training, management development, and organizational design. In some companies, they have organized their expertise as internal consultants capable of facilitating business strategy through "visioning" exercises and high-performance work teams.

Human resource professionals have championed the focus on "people-centricity." Initially, it was just a matter of ensuring that the right people with the right skills were in the right positions at the right times to guarantee business success. Seems simple enough, but managing such an intricate process of individual and corporate development is no small task. When it was realized that such expertise was necessary in order to create competitive advantage, executive leadership took notice of the challenge to be addressed.

What emerged is a new focus on learning, leadership, the role of corporate culture, and the value of cross-boundary interaction. The behavioral implications of business success became paramount with the emergence of networked organizations, cross-cultural diversity, and a new style of management that was less hierarchical and more process-driven. "Pay-for-performance" incentives took on new meaning as the effects of downsizing on company morale had to be offset with new ways to motivate employees.

Throughout the quality and reengineering efforts, the expertise of human resource professionals became essential to the process. Whether analyzing decision-making systems, managing conflict resolution, and/or aligning intellectual assets with the work (e.g., sourcing and outsourcing), organizations developed a new appreciation for interpersonal and group communications. Teams/teaming and human networks/networking are fundamental skills in a collaborative, interdependent global economy.

Response in the profession has been one of research in the learning process, institutes for human dynamics, centers for leadership development, career development tools, and a dedication to values, behavior, and results. In each of these areas, it has been the contribution from other functions and/or disciplines that has enhanced the capability of the human resource function itself. There are new positions, such as Chief Learning Officer, Chief Leadership Officer, and Chief Knowledge Officer—all of whom share a responsibility across the enterprise—the capacity to create and apply new ideas. In fact, at Nortel, Inc., the chief human resource officer is actually Vice President for Innovation Services.

Quality The (re)discovery of the importance of quality in products and services has provided all organizations—profit and not-for-profit—an enterprise-wide common agenda. Originating in the manufacturing community, the value of quality circles, statistical process control, and just-in-time methodologies swiftly spread through organizations. Incentives, such as the Baldrige Award, provided impetus to reach carefully defined standards. Winners were also quick to leverage their awards with marketing strategies to promote their industry leadership.

Organizations responded with assigning a Chief Quality Officer with budget and resources to create an infrastructure to manage the process. In fact, the focus on process—from supplier to customer delivery (i.e., the innovation process)—may be one of the major contributions of the field. This focus on the "end-to-end" process to determine value-added to the customer is precisely what helped organizations concentrate on the flow of materials into marketable products and processes.

The compounding effect was one of a learning environment. It was clear that there was a need for a training curriculum—and thereby a set of expert coaches; but the demonstrated effects of the training were in the "real-time" applications on the job. With this realization of the human aspects of the business, it was natural to refocus on the flow of knowledge and the measurement of the performance thereof.

The concept of benchmarking best practices is a major contribution to the field. Executives began to look across industry boundaries for examples of exemplary processes. Organizations such as the American Productivity and Quality Center (APQC) have seized the leadership in promoting a new awareness of the fundamental importance of the role of knowledge in sustaining business success and have developed a benchmarking capability to track the best knowledge management practices.

What began as a manufacturing focus quickly spread through every organization within the enterprise as well as the links with suppliers, partners, and—in some cases—distribution channels. The quality process transformed into the innovation process, in which reduced cycle time, organizational change, market positioning, and customer interaction are essential. The strategic concept of "designing for success" has significantly improved the innovation practices of most organizations.

Information Technology Perhaps no function has undergone more radical transformation than those responsible for the technical infrastructure. The average life span of a Chief Information Officer was/is less than two years.[4] Perhaps this is due to the explosion of advancements in the technology itself or is a function of the enterprise-wide responsibilities in the organization. The "productivity paradox" may play a role, as well as the level of importance placed on technology as the competitive weapon within a given industry.

Regardless, the response of the profession has been impressive. Similar to the human resource and quality professionals, the information technology specialists replicated the responsibility in every function and business unit in the enterprise. Furthermore, the spectrum of professional activities (e.g., meetings, roundtables, institutes, conferences, interest groups, etc.) includes—by definition—expert representatives from other functions. Quite naturally, because of their technical expertise, their knowledge base was global in scope.

As experts in systems, they have been systematic in their implementation to absorb and systematize the "torrents of technology" available. They have adopted a sophisticated educational program—electronic in some instances—to ensure optimal utilization of the technology. In fact, they have realized that the behavioral issues are equal in significance to any technical opportunities and must be addressed accordingly.

Technology serves as a competitive advantage in many dimensions: enabling the business, as a learning tool, accelerating the innovation cycle, etc. Somehow the explosion of technology tools (e.g., multimedia, large databases, data mining, intranetworking, conferencing, the Internet, et al.) must be deployed with a strategic vision in mind. Somehow, the complexity of the multitude of internal and external variables must be managed to the firm's advantage.

Internally, former information technology managers are finding themselves to be knowledge managers whose technical responsibilities are minuscule in comparison to their need to understand the business strategy, learning mechanisms, and overall organizational infrastructure. For many companies, this has evolved into a network of professionals with varied backgrounds who share a common purpose in the organization and beyond.

Response within the profession has been to embrace the knowledge agenda. Many CIOs have realized that their focus is not one of information technology, but the creation of an infrastructure to enable the flow of knowledge (i.e., information with meaning). Several have changed their titles to reflect the vision of the profession and are called Chief Technology Officers or Chief Innovation Officers. There is evidence that the Global Information Infrastructure may in actuality be a Global *Innovation* Infrastructure for moving good ideas around the world from point of creation to point of need.

R&D/Technology Transfer The function that previously maintained primary authority for innovation was R&D. Whether discussing invention or innovation, the research officers held the responsibility. As the distinction between invention and the full commercialization process occurred, some progressive managers assumed titles that reflected both research and business development—the vertical and horizontal responsibilities for the entire innovation process. Invention was openly the first phase. Interaction with all other functions and business units became essential. In this regard, R&D met the marketplace.

The research portfolio, in addition to expanding geographically, broadened to include the "soft sciences." Executives realized that the management of the technology was less developed than the technology itself. Companies joined in research consortia and university management research programs to bootstrap the capability of academicians and industrialists alike. In high-technology companies and economies, artificial intelligence had been funded as a technology in and of itself. When the general management sciences began to focus on the management of intellectual resources, a natural symbiosis was created between the two.

The technology transfer specialty was developed to optimize the flow of technology into and within the corporation. The focus soon became one of exchange in recognition of the dual communications nature of the process (i.e., ideas could/should come from each side). The shift from technology (e.g., technical reports, product prototypes, patents, etc.) to knowledge in the research process itself evolved from a realization that the process was one of human interactions, not discrete deliverables. Timely access to the knowledge (i.e., what works and what doesn't work) became more important than the deliverable research outcome itself.

Once it was clear that the process could not be left to serendipity, the field of knowledge management emerged as a new discipline with its own professional societies, advanced degree programs, and the founding of national and international centers for research and commercialization bridging the diverse but common needs of government, industry, and academe. Legislative initiatives promoted international competitiveness through the effective deployment of technology. Ultimately, these processes of innovation will operate as self-managing systems and virtual learning networks to ensure sustainable economic growth at every level. The agenda is one of transformation, not transfer.

Engineering Cross-functional management may have been first demonstrated in initiatives such as concurrent engineering and simultaneous development processes. Review of these progressive management approaches reveals that they may be innovation initiatives with another name. In order to effectively develop products, engineering managers realized that there was knowledge resident within the other sectors that was required for success. Most of the product development costs can be avoided if the information is known from the beginning and built into the design phase.

The concepts of engineering eventually migrated to other functions, such as Design for Manufacturing (DFM) and reengineering of the entire innovation process itself. In fact, the core principles of technical standards and architectures provide the foundation of what we know today as managerial architectures and managerial standards.

Engineers may have been the first users of computer systems in ways that leverage the power of computation technology. They also spearheaded the automation and integration of software tools (e.g., CAD/CAM, finite element analysis, rapid prototyping), which promoted sophisticated ways to enhance both the quality and speed to market.

Cross-disciplinary research between engineering and computer science initiated some integrated programs that enhanced the acceleration of transformation of the function. Initiatives began to spawn outcomes of mega-magnitude previously unimaginable (e.g., use of computers in finite element analysis, Computer-Aided Design and Computer-Aided Manufacturing, robotics, supercomputers, complex engineering calculations, and statistical process control).

At the same time, companies were experimenting with new organizational reporting structures in which engineering and manufacturing functions were integrated. Simultaneously, the focus on low-cost manufacturing evolved into a focus on lowest-cost development.

As a profession, engineering addressed the issues of availability of knowledge and know-how in a future workforce. The National Academy of Engineering and societies in the engineering professions (e.g., the American Society for Engineering Education, IEEE, ACM, et al.) created the National Congress on Engineering Education, the first effort of its kind to identify the key issues in the profession and potential strategies.[5] The task forces provided opportunities across functional, sector, and industry boundaries, leading to a greater understanding of one another's competencies.

Manufacturing The integration of technology push and market pull (i.e., supply/demand, needs/seeds) ultimately takes place in the manufacturing function—or the translation phase of the process of innovation. With intensified global competition and companies that were more expert at commercializing technology—even from other countries—focus on the production aspects of goods and services became paramount.

Previously relegated to third-class citizenship on the corporate ladder—and in the professional schema—manufacturing engineers were put to the test. Not only were they able to display their prowess with statistical analysis, but being the first to embrace the quality agenda enabled them to provide corporate leadership in team building as well as in customer interaction. Instead of being perceived at the end of the value chain, customers were perceived as at the heart of the Quality Function Deployment (QFD) process.

Across the nation—and indeed the world—there was an intensified focus on the manufacturing sector of the economy and its role in international competition. There was an appreciation for the conversion process within traditional industries, the services sector, and the newly transformed federal laboratories.

What emerged was an intensive movement to promote corporate agility that had its roots in the manufacturing sector. Today, the Agility Forum (it has dropped the word manufacturing from its title), which is based at Lehigh University, boasts a significant cross-industry membership, with research initiatives ranging from change management to "Next Generation Manufacturing: Plan for Action." Its conference agenda, similar to that of other manufacturing forums (e.g., the National Center for Manufacturing Sciences, the Center for International Manufacturing Systems), resembles that of an organization dedicated to the process of innovation. They have even produced an imperative paper on "Innovation Process," which builds a bridge between technological innovation and the learning process.

Marketing/Planning If R&D has historically been responsible for innovation from the invention phase of the process, Marketing has been responsible for the commercialization phase. In this respect, business development has been the domain of market research professionals. With markets forming and reforming at a blistering pace, the role has increased over time. Magnified market fragmentation and the need for relational marketing have created kaleidoscopic dynamics that defy precise market forecasting. Sophisticated communications strategies (e.g., multiple media, role of the business and trade press, leveraged public relations, etc.) help manage the pace of global change.

With the importance of projecting future strategies through the planning process, managers must become more sophisticated in defining new business opportunities and monitoring the competitors, including those who may not be competitors today. The new orientation is one of leveraging competencies to meet the unarticulated needs of customers and unserved markets. Marketing professionals have realized that value of innovating with the customer as a way to differentiate themselves from the competition and leverage distinct competencies.

The shift has been from a focus on plans to the enterprise-wide innovation process itself. In fact, the entire field of strategic planning has recently transformed into one of leadership. Even the Strategic Planning Forum (i.e., the planning officers of the major corporations worldwide) became the Strategic Leadership Forum in 1996. Rather than tracking past market trends and building forecasts based on an extrapolation of current budgets, planning officials are experimenting with intensive group learning exercises, such as scenario planning.

This revised charter, together with the uncertainties of the economy, demands knowledge from all functions, business units, and geographies in order to develop an effective enterprise leadership strategy. There is a new appreciation of competitive intelligence and, in some instances, collaborative intelligence. How does one develop a rationale and business plan for a market that doesn't exist today, but is likely to form overnight? Traditional mechanisms and metrics will not suffice.

Sales/Services The services sector has become the fastest-growing sector of economies around the world as a percentage of GNP. At the same time, the services function within the manufacturing sector has become an integral part of the innovation system, since professionals are the closest to the point of customer interface. Indeed, in several industries, service—as opposed to products per se—is becoming the business as base hardware and software are provided free of charge in order to gain profit margins from service revenue.

The cost of goods sold has significantly increased over the past few years due to the complexity of the marketplace, the difficulty in justifying distinctive advantages, and the base cost of related resources. Another contributing factor is the lengthened sales cycle due to increased difficulty in decision-making. All these issues require that the sales and service personnel rely on knowledge and expertise from several other functional competencies (e.g., R&D, engineering, manufacturing, et al.) in the organization in order to make the sale.

Companies have shifted toward telemarketing strategies, but even those can be costly. There is a need to understand and fully utilize multiple channels of distribution in order to maintain market flexibility. The experimental growth of electronic commerce on the World Wide Web has provided a new mechanism for promoting products and services to a worldwide clientele.

As modern concepts of customer partnering evolve, the sales and service functions will change dramatically. Instead of being at the end of the value chain, they will be portrayed as the lead agents for learning from the customers and feeding that insight back through the innovation functions of the company.

Alliances/Joint Ventures The newest function in the innovation spectrum, managers of corporate alliances have been established as a necessity in an era of collaborative strategy. No longer can organizations manage the economic dynamics alone. There are many who believe that, in the future, companies will be measured as sets of alliances against other sets of alliances. True or not, companies are expanding the scope of their stakeholders to include companies and other organizations as an integral part of their corporate strategy.

As the value system becomes bundled—or unbundled, as the case may be—there is a recognition that these new partnerships must be managed. Goals and expectations must be carefully articulated. Values and cultures must be in sync. Performance must be measured and periodic adjustments made to plans.

A respect for complementary competencies must exist within and throughout the strategic business network to optimize results. The partnership must be balanced, except in the case of mergers, and even then, attention must be given to the process of integration along multiple managerial dimensions. The dynamics of the marketplace are likely to place continuing demands on a variety of ways to share expertise across organization borders (e.g., outsourcing, joint marketing, shared distribution systems, etc.).

Although a new focus in corporate management, alliance managers are experts in managing complexity and market potential. They know how to combine resources in ways that can create distinctive competencies. They also understand how to manage the relationship through effective communications. They will have to become more expert at justifying the intangible assets in the relationship. How can you establish an alliance that promotes an optimal flow of knowledge, but maintains the proprietary information within the company that makes it competitive?

Today, innovation is coming from every segment of corporate management. *Finance* managers are recognizing the need to measure the intangibles. *Human resource* managers are equipped to provide the leadership around learning networks and the flow of knowledge through education and development initiatives. The chief *information* officer is now knowledgeable about the behavioral aspects of the technology as well as the new intelligence and communications capabilities. They are also familiar with the need to support the entire corporation.

The *marketing* staff has developed sophisticated mechanisms to track trends and forecast them forward in ways that might help you generate new markets and even transform your industry. The *quality* experts have carefully defined the intricacies of all the processes involved in managing the business from supplier to consumer.

The *R&D* staff, which is expert in the invention stage of the process of innovation, has now developed new skills in business development. The *engineering* staff has applied its technical rigor to the entire system of innovation through concurrent engineering. The *manufacturing* experts have done the same through the concepts of agile manufacturing. The planning processes are now as important as the plans, and the new forms of strategy are actually leadership-based more than product- or market-oriented. The *public relations* staff has created an integrated communications strategy to continue your leadership position and capitalize on the variety of media available. The *sales* staff has realized the value of its positioning with the customer and has developed innovative ways to tap into the knowledge source and feed those insights directly to your R&D staff. *Services* have become the business in terms of profitability and added value.

This is the rich expertise available as you chart an innovation course forward. All that is left to do is to bring together those diverse perspectives and leverage the complementary expertise of your leadership team. Innovation strategy may be the one way to create a simple solution amid all the complexity.

Summary

Every function has undergone dramatic change over the past few years—as a function, as a profession, and as a collection of expertise across traditional boundaries. Each has learned from the others and contributed to their body of knowledge. Individual communities of practice have evolved on virtually every topic imaginable. It is this cross-boundary sharing and learning that is accelerating the momentum of progress. This is precisely the reason that the knowledge movement is fundamental, not a fad.

Only a few years ago, the fortresses between the functions could have been miniature Chinese Great Walls. Today—corporate politics notwithstanding—they are collaborators in new innovation systems based on the ability to create and move ideas into the marketplace. They have discovered the value of their complementary competencies and how they contribute to the whole. With a shared purpose, they are moving toward a common strategic vision. In the process, they are unleashing the creativity in organizations. What they share in common is more important than their differences; and they are all active participants in this rapidly maturing *community of knowledge practice.*

Notes

1. John Seely Brown and Estee Solomon Gray, "After Re-Engineering: The People Are The Company." *FAST Company* 1, no. 1 (Premier Issue 1995): 78–82.
2. March 1996, a *New York Times* survey.
3. Canadian Institute of Certified Public Accountants.
4. *ComputerWorld*, September 16, 1996, pp. 88-89.
5. *Report of the National Congress on Engineering Education*. Published by the American Society for Engineering Education.
6. "Innovation Process," an imperative paper sponsored by the Next Generation Manufacturing (NGM) Project (Bethlehem, PA: The Agility Forum, Lehigh University, 1997).

5

Innovation as a Value System

Smart infrastructures
provide the freedom to come and go,
capacity to accelerate the flow of information,
ability to speed the use of technology,
capability to reduce development time
and flexibility to allow for
a culture and environment
that encourages and rewards innovation.
—DR. GEORGE KOZMETSKY[1]

If you ask employees throughout an organization how they rate themselves according to their capacity to create new ideas, the response, which we will call the *Idea Creativity Quotient*, is likely to be quite high. Usually 95 percent of the people will rate themselves a 7 or above on a scale of 1 to 10. If you ask the same group to rate their ability to know what to do with those good ideas, invariably 50 percent of the hands go down, indicating a lower *Quality Quotient*. Finally, if you ask them to rate their faith that their good ideas will end up in marketable products and services that will benefit the enterprise, few employees—even members of the leadership team—rate themselves very high. Virtually all hands are down. This, of course, indicates a woefully low *Innovation Quotient*, which is precisely the capability needed to compete in the future.

Due to severe restructuring, downsizing, and reengineering initiatives, most companies have realized that they have lost the capacity to innovate. They are too lean. Henry Conn, an executive at A.T. Kearney, describes this as "corporate anorexia."[2] Theresa Amabile, a Harvard professor, has documented the effects of downsizing on creativity in an article in *Research in Organizational Behavior*.[3] There is evidence that risk has been squeezed out of the system with excruciating cost-reduction programs. In many cases, progressive managers have left their companies on their own initiative. Experimentation is considered a luxury. Long-term programs have lower priority than activities that produce short-term profits to satisfy Wall Street.

Most senior managers recognize their need to balance the strategic and operational foci in the organization. They juggle investments for the long and short terms. They understand that organizations must be networked, but must have decision-making processes in place for appropriate control. The real dilemma for senior management, however, is how best to manage the innovation capability of an organization in an environment that seems to dampen creativity and even responsible risk-taking.

The innovation process should be made explicit from the beginning. All constituents ought to understand their contribution to the process and how best to create value-added. The defined values of the company should include statements and actions that support creativity and innovation. Incentives should make valuable contributions visible and motivate employees at every level to participate in the process.

Gauging the Organization

One barometer for how innovative your organization is can be obtained by answering the following questions with a *yes* or *no* in the box provided.

	YES	NO
1. Has one person been chartered with the overall responsibility to manage the corporate-wide innovation process?	☐	☐
2. Are there performance measures—both tangible and intangible—to assess the quality of your innovation practices?	☐	☐

	YES	NO
3. Do your training/educational programs have provisions to incubate and spin out new products and businesses?	☐	☐
4. Does your local, regional, or international presence operate as a distributed network of expertise that learns from as well as distributes to customers?	☐	☐
5. Is there a formal intelligence-gathering strategy to monitor the positioning of both current and potential competitors?	☐	☐
6. Does the rate of production of new products and services exceed the norms of your industry and create new markets in which you can excel?	☐	☐
7. Has a strategic alliance manager been designated to create and manage the network of partnerships and joint ventures to leverage your firm?	☐	☐
8. Does your marketing image portray an organization with the capacity to create and move ideas into the marketplace to make your customers successful?	☐	☐
9. Have resources been allocated to articulate a compelling vision internally and share company expertise externally through publications and participation in major forums?	☐	☐
10. Is your computer/communications capability treated as a learning tool for internal conferencing and external business leverage on the World Wide Web?	☐	☐

If you answered 7 out of the 10 questions in the affirmative, the chances are that you have a good handle on the innovation process of your enterprise and know how to enable an environment for the optimal flow of ideas contributing to the vitality of the company. However, if you found yourself responding negatively to these basic innovation questions, you may want to take a look at your own processes for taking ideas to market and leveraging your intellectual capability into the future.

For most organizations, the *Innovation Quotient* is dangerously low. Over the years, the nature of the budgeting process, for both private and public institutions, has fostered attitudes and practices of competition. (*Note:* Interestingly enough, the word processor thesaurus presents *complaint* as a substitute for the word *competition*.) This is not necessarily a problem when resources are abundant and the market offers significant growth to all. But when resources become constrained and hypercompetitive markets are the norm, organizations must fuse their interests and expertise for the good of the organization. It is the only strategy for providing "more for less."

Believe it or not, the most precious resource that organizations are now trying to manage is "knowledge-space." Leadership is bombarded with competing and often conflicting major initiatives to move the organization forward. Even in a networked society, there is still a need for hierarchical endorsement in order for any stream of activity to flourish. Command-and-control management has not been replaced with a totally free enterprise model for obvious reasons; but the "control" aspects have been replaced by the concepts of managerial guidance, coaching, direction, and accountability. It is the metaphor of the orchestra leader rather than the decision-making czar; and it is demonstrated as vision and strategy are crafted, not dictated.

Coming Together

As an example, let us review a plausible scenario. The chief executive officer is bombarded with ideas and requests from the leadership team to assure the company's prosperity. Unless there is an extraordinary group of managers, they are usually promoting solutions from their particular field of expertise:

The *finance* manager says to downsize, manage productivity, cut costs, and maximize ROI. The *human resource* manager says your people are the most valuable asset and should be treated as an investment, not an expense. The *education/training* professionals agree and promote learning networks throughout the company. The chief *information* officer says investing in the technology infrastructure is fundamental to your competitive future.

The *marketing* manager advises a focus on the planning process, not the plans per se, and points out that the competition includes companies you haven't considered in your recent analysis. If there is an *alliance* manager, he or she tries to convey an understanding that only through collaborative ventures can the business effectively grow. Even partnering with customers is essential. The chief *quality* officer says there is an opportunity to win the Baldrige Award if the full leadership team makes the commitment to quality initiatives.

The *R&D* officer says that without research investments commensurate with industry norms, the company will not have the products and services to compete in the future. The chief e*ngineer* says that you must institute cross-functional, simultaneous development processes. The *manufacturing* officer explains that the company must become more "agile"—flexible in its processes along the entire value chain (i.e., essentially the same message as that of the engineering staff).

The *public relations/communications* expert says that progressive messages must be aligned in a systematic campaign across multiple media. The *sales* executives say that current products and services are not reaching the marketplace in a timely manner nor at competitive prices. The *service* managers describe the difficulty of being at the end of the food chain when—in fact—they are closest to the needs of the customers and should be utilized accordingly.

Meanwhile, the *competition* seems to be able to bring ideas to market at a faster pace and with greater quality. *Suppliers* are trying to provide advice because their success has become dependent on the prosperity of your company. *Customers* want to remain loyal, but are having difficulty lobbying on your behalf inside their own companies.

They all could be right because these statements represent the current thinking in their respective professions as well as the realities of the hypercompetitive marketplace. We learned in chapter 4 that communities of practice are beginning to bridge the chasms between the functions, but most organizations still represent *third-generation management,* in which collaboration is structured at best (i.e., not self-organizing).

What should the CEO do? Where is the commonality in all these observations? What is the fundamental core that brings each one to the boardroom with his or her complementary competency? How might all this diverse expertise be harnessed in ways that will ensure the profitable success of the firm? It matters not whether you are a start-up company or a large-scale enterprise, the challenge is the same: innovate or close up shop.

Creation of an innovation strategy may be the bonding initiative that creates the common language, capitalizes on distinctive competencies, and fuses collective knowledge into a shared purpose. However, few organizations have an explicit innovation process—never mind a designated senior executive responsible for oversight of that process. The fact remains that the chief executive is the one ultimately responsible for ensuring sustained profitable growth throughout the entire idea-to-market cycle. The truth is that every competence in the organization must play a role, but often these roles and their interdependence lack definition for efficient management.

Transition from Value Chain to Integrated System

Michael Porter, a Harvard professor, made a major contribution to the field by outlining the managerial concepts inherent in the *value chain*.[4] Although he defined innovation in terms of technological change, the construct he developed is still utilized today as managers attempt to systematically divide the firm into discrete activities. It was designed as a basic tool for diagnosing competitive advantage and discovering ways to create and sustain it. Porter did cite the need for creating and managing linkages among organizational units as an important issue in the implementation of strategy. However, his illustrations remained linear in design and unidirectional even as he expanded his view of the value system for a diversified firm that included value chains for suppliers, channels, and buyers.

With the advent of learning systems and networked organizations and the adoption of systems dynamics principles espoused by Jay W. Forrester, an MIT professor, we are able to gain a more dynamic perspective on innovation strategy as a value system of interdependent activities influencing and being influenced by one another.[5] Thanks to the simplicity defined by Porter, we are in a better position to understand the complexity of the modern-day enterprise.

This refocus, although necessary, is still difficult to comprehend. It requires a view of the organization as a whole prior to understanding the interrelationship of its parts. This holistic management can bridge Eastern and Western thought into portraits of value creation through integration and ultimate innovation. In Monet's terms, it is stepping back from the canvas—which heretofore has been covered with meticulous strokes of detail (i.e., the statistical process control and short-term financial rigor of the quality/reengineering era). Instead, it is time to revisit the entire spectrum of possibility in order to define an effective strategy forward.

Figures 5–1 and 5–2 may help in visualizing the difference in a chain versus a system. Figure 5–1 illustrates the basic functions in the value chain similar to what Porter described in the early 1980s. This is one way to view the entire spectrum of activities that are described by a variety of leading authorities in the field.

Some will describe the concept of idea generation through market diffusion. Bruce Merrifield, as described in chapter 3, segmented the three stages of the process as invention, translation, and commercialization. One major consulting firm has described it as a sequence of four processes: discovery, investigation, development, and launch. Academi-

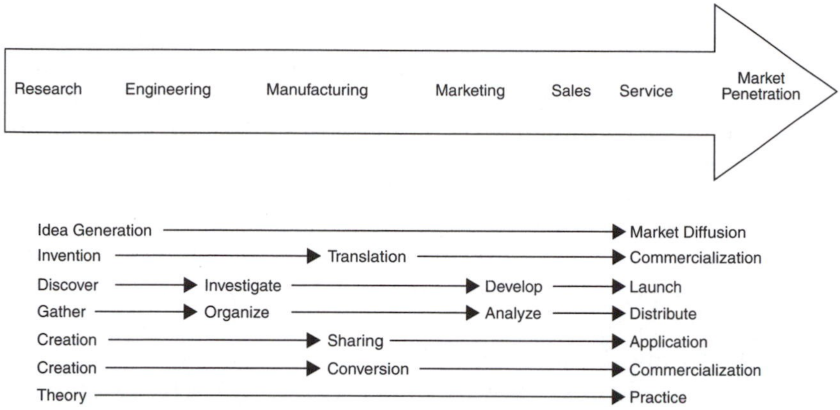

Figure 5–1 The Innovation Value Chain.

cians have used the terms gather, organize, analyze, and distribute. In the knowledge management field, it is described as creation, sharing, and application. My own distinctions, which are all interdependent, define the 3C's: Creation, Conversion, and Commercialization. Basically, all descriptions are referring to the full innovation process as a way to integrate theory and practice.

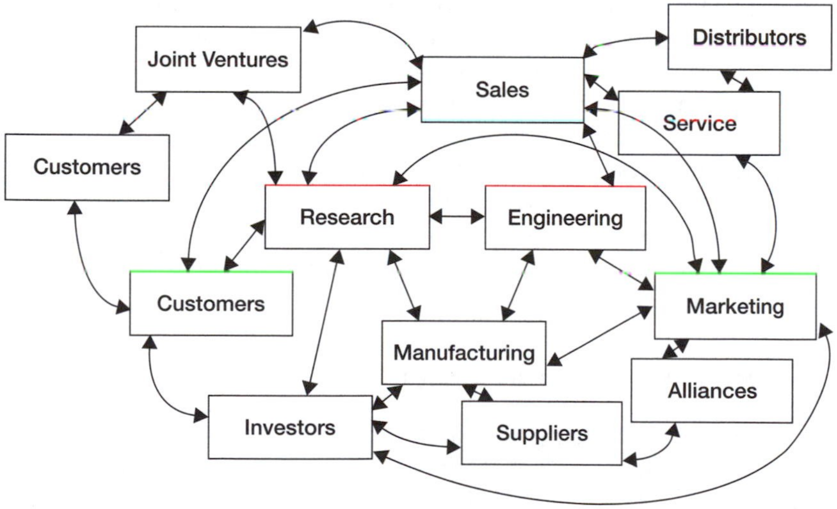

Figure 5–2 The Innovation Value System.

By examining this chain, you can envision how the expansion of R&D responsibilities to include business development is really *innovation* with a capital *R*. The notions of concurrent engineering are really *innovation* with a capital *E*. Agile manufacturing is really *innovation* with a capital *M*. New initiatives in collaborative sales and services are really *innovation* with a capital *S*. Even the TQM movement can be portrayed as *innovation* with a capital *Q*. There will be other examples as communities of practice begin to broaden their spheres of influence. If all these initiatives can be recognized as innovation strategy, then the leadership can begin to capitalize on the diverse complementary competencies that can be brought to bear.

If this view is not revolutionary enough, then take the leap of faith into the world of systems dynamics (Figure 5-2), which values the interdependencies within the functions and the dual communication nature of the innovation process. In other words, ideas may—and must—flow from anywhere in the value system. Expertise and activities in one function may affect several other functions simultaneously. The knowledge gleaned from a customer at the point of delivery may have as much value for the research into new product development as it has for sales and marketing. This notion can be adapted in the non-profit sector as well, as organizations convert to a success rather than satisfaction model of customer interaction.

Today, value-chain thinking is simplistic and inadequate. Although originally useful in defining linear relationships and discrete activities, it does not provide a robust framework for modern innovation strategy, which capitalizes on the strength of a networked enterprise and the knowledge-based firm. It hardly provides for the real-time decision-making demanded by a kaleidoscopic marketplace; nor does it allow for optimal resource integration from a global perspective. The interdependent knowledge economy demands a more fluid management system to enable highly leveraged business decisions. As incomplete as is the value system described above, it does represent some of the possibilities afforded by a different view of the management structure and the linkages among the parts.

Ken of Innovation in Practice: Analog Devices

It is one thing to define theoretical foundations, identify prevailing principles, and draw graphic diagrams to simulate desirable interactions among functions, but how do these concepts play out in actuality? One case of exemplary innovation practice was featured in the June 1996 issue of *Knowledge Inc.*[6] With permission, the case is profiled here.

Analog Devices Invests in Intellectual Assets

When you hear about chief executives trying to "transform" their organizations, you can expect them to be under financial duress or in the midst of some other organizational crisis. One corporate leader who considers transformation to be an ongoing effort, who isn't waiting for a crisis, is Ray Stata, Chairman and CEO of Norwood-based Analog Devices. The company, which has invested heavily in the development of its intellectual capital, has consistently demonstrated strong financial performance.

Indeed, Analog Devices may now be stronger than ever. The firm, which designs and manufactures integrated circuits that are employed in signal processing applications, saw sales increase 22 percent to $942 million in fiscal year 1995. Net income rose 60 percent to $119.3 million. Financials for the first half of 1996—profits climbed 70 percent to $40.1 million in the first quarter and 53 percent to $44 million in the second—suggest that the company will have another stellar year.

Such performance gains can be largely attributed to the company's conscious efforts to develop a shared vision and common language that facilitates continuous learning.

"The roots of this new thinking are based in organizational theory and the recognition that learning and improvement are two sides of the same coin," Stata told me in a recent interview. "We are all experiencing the same phenomenon and recognizing that something fundamental is happening."

"For Analog, it was easy to apply Total Quality Management as the starting place," he added. "We used the concepts to create a common commitment to the notion of quality." Stata, who has worked closely with the Center for Quality Management (CQM), an organization closely affiliated with MIT, explains that TQM has evolved as a discipline in recent years. "There has been a shift from the quality of products to the quality of services and ultimately to the quality of management," he says. "How the concepts and methodologies are applied within Analog has paralleled this transition."

As an illustration of how Analog has developed its common language and framework, he explained that all six members of his executive management team had initially participated in a week-long course sponsored by CQM. "The value was one of total participation," he says, explaining that all of the managers explored what they could do for continuous learning which included both incremental and breakthrough improvements.

This is consistent with what John Seely Brown, Director of Xerox PARC, defines as a "community of practice"—peers in the execution of "real work," held together by a common sense of purpose and a real need to know what each other knows. In the case of Analog, Stata was able to establish that sense of collaborative commitment with the executive management team. The common bond was the quest for highly effective learning.

Such activities have clearly made an impact on the organization. The company's CFO, for instance, has aggressively pursued a quality agenda in an effort to transform internal financial and accounting services. As part of his efforts, he benchmarked and developed predictive metrics to gauge improvement. He focused on the total organizational structure and processes within the system. He also redesigned the planning framework for finance to facilitate the delivery of information beyond the traditional financial data—and to strengthen his group's role as a service provider to internal customers.

It's clear that cross-functional collaboration is valued at Analog. The responsibilities that the finance manager had assumed, in this case, ordinarily might have been confined to the chief information officer or even the human resource professional. In developing a common language, however, the company appears to have generated respect for the complementary competencies that exist internally. In this way, the team of expertise is harnessed toward a common strategic vision as a collective of knowledge. Each contributes—from its own perspective—to the value of the whole.

Stata, who has authored two books on innovation (*Global Stakes* and *The Innovators*) and has been an active promoter of organizational learning since his influential article on the subject in the *Sloan Management Review* in 1989, contends the most significant challenge facing companies committed to learning, quality and cross-functional leadership is one of momentum. He says that it has been important to emphasize to his workforce that sustaining continuous improvement alone is not enough—even when or especially when things are going well.

In presentations to his employees and meetings with his management team, he has tried to encourage the development of a "community of inquirers" rather than a "community of advocates." It is a different mindset, he explains. Rather than forcing ideas on one another, employees are encouraged to understand and leverage each other's knowledge, skills, experience and diversity of views.

Influenced by the work of management theorist Fernando Flores, Stata has often described his organization as a "network of conversations." While decision-making is a critical aspect of management, he points out that coordinating and meeting commitments is the primary role of managers; and conversation skills—both listening and speaking—are the means by which concerns and conflicts are resolved, agreements on goals are reached and goals are ultimately accomplished.

Indeed, he believes it is vital to improve the quality of both conversations and relationships in the organization. "With a little coaching and feedback, you will be surprised by how much what you say and how you say it affects the quality of your relationships and the effectiveness of your management style," he contends.

He also makes a distinction between accountability—that which you have promised or committed to do—and responsibility. Responsibility, he maintains, is a commitment to mutual achievement. "To build high-quality relationships in the work environment, we must each be committed to each other's success," he told his employees in one presentation. "In this kind of relationship, when something is really important, we go beyond the contractual conditions of satisfaction of our promises and do whatever is necessary to achieve a successful outcome."

And while he believes that quality and reengineering efforts have enabled companies to improve efficiency, he thinks they have not encouraged the effectiveness that is needed to compete in a dynamic marketplace. "This requires much more creative integration of the right market strategies with market needs," he explains. In this respect, the management challenge of the decade is defined: How do we maintain continuous capacity for innovation that enables sustained, profitable growth? The answers may not be found in Analog's integrated circuit technologies per se, but in the management thereof.

Of course, information technologies will continue to play a role in the knowledge sharing, creation and management necessary to enhance organizational learning at Analog. The firm makes content about best practices available to everyone in the company via its local area network. It also provides software tools—such as "product start documents" and a "product information cost system"—that enable chip developers to glean important "learnings" from previous product generations and, thereafter, determine how to most effectively design and develop the ICs.

The company also is an aggressive user of email and increasingly, Lotus Notes. In fact, its 200-plus member sales force is committed to using Notes worldwide as a vehicle to incorporate division, marketing and engineering resources to cut time-to-market. Customer-specific information is then extracted and placed in the firm's Sales and Marketing Information System. This allows internal market strategists to leverage the lessons learned in the market, which are stored in the SMIS database, to create the strategic goals and actions necessary to reach markets effectively in the future. That's vital. Robert Stasey, the company's director of quality improvement, explains that Analog "is basically a new product engine. Life cycles are short and we want to obsolete our own products before the competition does."

Such improvements and innovations, concludes Stata, depend on effective collaboration. He argues that "the single spear carrier"—the individual—can no longer "slay the dragon." It is the collective knowledge and action which brings about the innovation necessary to compete. Only when the competencies are aligned—working synergistically—can tangible benefits be derived.

One management problem that most companies now face is that groups with different competencies compete internally for the same resources—financial, and more importantly mindshare of the leadership. They should instead be establishing an innovation strategy whereby all competencies can be jointly mobilized to capitalize on the opportunities afforded by unarticulated needs and unserved markets.

Analog Devices, which has focused on the nature of its "conversations" and the collaboration between various functional groups, offers a strong example of what can be achieved. Just look at the numbers.

Redefining the Boundaries of the Enterprise

No enterprise is an island—especially in the knowledge economy. As necessary as corporate walls may be for the purpose of measuring and reporting P&L statements, the reality is that the flow of knowledge must transcend traditional organization boundaries and include sources of knowledge from all stakeholders, including suppliers, alliances, distributors, customers, and even competitors. This new definition of the Strategic Business Network (SBN) will be described in more detail in chapter 6.

What has been described in Figures 5-1 and 5-2 represents the intra-organization structure of the innovation process. It illustrates the *internal* functioning of the organization, which has been the primary focus of many restructuring efforts. Given the dynamics of the economy, the real opportunity lies with how effectively organizations are able to interface with the *external* relationships. Real value is created with what we will call *knowledge fusion* across organizational boundaries. As Sheridan Tatsuno described in *Created in Japan*:

> Western creativity is based on the notion of individual freedom and expression. It is like nuclear fission in which individual atoms produced energy; by contrast Japanese creativity is more like nuclear fusion, in which particles must join together in order to create a reaction.[7]

As firms adapt to more networked organizations and as the utilization of communications technology accelerates, organizations will discover more effective ways to unleash continuous creativity. It is this entrepreneurial collaboration from idea creation to prosperous application that will sustain the viability of a company, an industry, or a nation.

The evolution of "lotus innovation" thinking is described in a 1991 presentation that I made in Lyons, France.[8] It begins with the value chain used at the 1987 Roundtable, "Managing the Knowledge Asset into the 21st Century." In this technology transfer continuum, the focus was on how best to bring knowledge and technology into the corporation from university and research laboratories. Even with this diagram, traditional value-chain theories were challenged. The nature of the process meant fuzzy boundaries between the functions as notions of what, how, and when to transfer technology were questioned. The graphic also depicts a dual communication (i.e., not unidirectional) process in which industry has as much to offer academe as the reverse. It also represents the thinking that ideas can—and indeed must—originate from everywhere in the corporation. And finally, one has not innovated until the market demands more of the technology developed.

An examination of the technology transfer processes of effective Japanese firms made visible the value-added positioning of customers at the front end of the value chain, as illustrated by NEC's value links. Quality methodologies positioned customers—appropriately so—at the heart of the innovation process, in which all functions determine activities based on value added to the customer.

It was only one step, then, to create a Venn diagram to illustrate the integration of the value-system functions into what constitutes the first tier of the "innovation lotus flower" outlined in my published MIT thesis, *Global Innovation Strategy: Creating Value-Added Alliances.* This still represents only the *microeconomic,* intra-organization interactions needed for cross-functional teaming and enterprise-wide alignment. Although the work of the functions themselves will continue to remain an integral functioning of an organization, the real value-added comes from the cross-boundary integration that occurs in the name of progress.

To focus solely internally is naive. Time-to-market efficiencies can come only from taking advantage of external expertise. The second tier of the lotus innovation flower is formed with those relationships that must network outside expertise with internal sources who are at the point of need or vice versa. In this regard, the *mesoeconomic* level (i.e., suppliers, partners, education, government, distributors, and other stakeholders) becomes a part of the living human and technical network of the organization. In some respects, competitors in and across industries become allies, and in some respects former allies become competitors. The knowledge base now expands to include all connections as potential sources of knowledge for added value.

In a transnational economy, the *macroeconomic,* networked connections must be managed simultaneously. All the economies of the world are potential conduits to the symbiotic partnering essential for company success. Organizations must assess, in Pogo's terms, the "insurmountable opportunities" afforded a global, borderless economy. In this regard, the third tier of the innovation flower—when viewed holistically—represents the optimal international infrastructure for the flow of knowledge. In some respects, critical questions must be raised for an organization seeking to position itself internationally: How will the workforce change to meet the fluctuating demographics? How can the company meet the rapidly evolving complex demands of a customer base expanding internationally? How can core company messages be delivered around the globe with timely cross-organizational processes? At the heart of all interactions is the concept of "innovating our future...together."

The resulting lotus innovation flower with its three tiers (i.e., microeconomic, mesoeconomic, and macroeconomic) provides a coherent planning framework in which an organization can consider its strategic vision. It incorporates the complex array of interactions necessary within the firm, outside the firm, and around the globe. As organizations continue to transcend boundaries of every dimension and the technology affords us communications opportunities previously unimaginable, the differences between us as companies, sectors, industries, and nations will disappear.

Where Does One Begin?

If you accept the notion that innovation strategy might be the rubric within which you can lead your organization forward, there are some simple steps to take:

Step 1: Make innovation (i.e., idea to market) an explicit and widely communicated strategy.

Step 2: Assign someone the responsibility/authority for the corporate-wide innovation process.

Step 3: Perform an honest assessment of your own innovation capacity to create and move ideas into the marketplace.

Step 4: Create a collaborative initiative that binds the whole enterprise, including all stakeholders (e.g., partners, suppliers, customers, and even competitors).

Step 5: Monitor your own progress against goals consistent with your corporate culture and practice the art of constructive (re)design.

This action plan itself need not be linear and should include feedback loops through the process to enhance quality and effectiveness. Most of all, the process should be one way management can begin to balance the short- and long-term objectives through an integrated program for business operations and strategy development.

Summary

The innovation process as newly defined is critical to the successful functioning of any organization in the future. It is the one competence needed to optimize results in the next millennium. It cannot be left to chance. Now, we have a way to view the future of the business regardless of the perspective from which we come. All of us have a way to contribute to the increased intellectual wealth of the enterprise that will have an impact in meaningful ways.

The economic kaleidoscope, if it is to be prosperous, must be managed. Modern philosophy and practice must eliminate unnecessary boundaries across functions, industries, sectors, or countries. Only through collaborative interaction will we be able to generate a shared prosperity for all.

Notes

1. George Kozmetsky, *IC^2 Annual Report* (Austin, Texas, 1991).
2. Bernard Wysocki, "Big Corporate Layoffs Are Slowing Down," *Wall Street Journal*, June 12, 1995, p. 1.
3. Theresa Amabile, "A Model of Creativity and Innovation in Organizations," in *Research in Organizational Behavior*, Barry Taw and Larry Cummings, eds. (JAI Press. vol. 10, 1988).
4. Michael Porter, *Competitive Advantage: Creating and Sustaining Superior Performance* (New York: The Free Press, 1985).
5. Jay W. Forrester, *Industrial Dynamics* (Cambridge, MA: MIT Press, 1985).
6. Debra M. Amidon Rogers, "Analog Devices Invests in Intellectual Assets," *Knowledge Inc.* vol. 1, no. 2 (June 1996).
7. Sheridan Tatsuno, *Created in Japan: From Imitators to World Class Innovators* (New York: Harper Business-Ballinger, 1990).
8. Debra M. Amidon Rogers, "Creating a Global Innovation Management System," in *Proceedings of the Grande Colloque de Perspective* (Ministry of Research, France, 1991).

6

An Innovation Management Architecture

Conventionally,
the logic of strategy has been predominantly that of economics:
demand, market competition, capital investment, production.
It has been mostly analytical.

The three elements [are] especially important:
the logic of invisible asset accumulation and utilization;
the logic of dynamic, unbalanced growth;
and the logic of human psychology—
both within the firm
and in dealings with customers
and competitors.

The holistic approach, integrating both types, is indispensable.
—Hiroyuki Itami [1]

"An architecture for management, you say?"

"Yes, that's what we need. The findings of the Roundtable indicate that technology is not the problem; the *management* of the technology is.

Even the most progressive research in the business schools does not begin to address the types of managerial issues we are confronting daily. Each one seems to have a piece of the puzzle, but no one understands the total management system."

"So you think you can apply technical theory to the concepts of management?" There is chuckling among the eleven senior engineering managers who are confronted with this opportunity.

"What makes you think there is any similarity in design?"

"I'm not sure. That's precisely what we need to learn. I would like to apply the same industrial research rigor we apply to the development of technical architectures and technical standards to the process of management. Do you believe it is possible?"

"Possible, not probable."

So went the 1986 discussion as I presented the case for a Management Systems Research (MSR) focus to the Sponsored Research Board of a major computer company. In the months that ensued, we explored all previous taxonomies for business management from corporate, consulting, and academic sources all over the world.

Thanks to Dr. Ron Smart, who managed the MSR laboratory, and Dr. Carl F. Cargill, the company's standards architect, we were able to identify the primary elements of the architecture and the rationale for creating worldwide standards. In fact, Cargill's book, *Information Technology Standardization: Theory, Process and Organizations,*[2] helped define the elements of the Prospectus for the Future represented in chapter 10.

Our technical architectures had served us well. Numerous other functions and businesses had initiated various architectural frameworks as a way of structuring the work. They provided a systematic way of visualizing technical business and planning processes. What was needed was an overarching managerial architecture that was simple—but not simplistic—that would harness the multiple interdependent business activities into an optimized human and technological system.

What evolved was an Enterprise Management System Architecture (which has since been relabeled Innovation Architecture), which can be summarized as five interrelated dimensions of the organization: *performance, structure, people, process,* and *technology.* This cross-disciplinary approach is one way to integrate the *economic, behavioral,* and *technological* aspects of the firm. For starters, we asked five basic questions about the functioning of the enterprise:

A. What will we MEASURE to assess goodness in performance results or plans?
B. How will we STRUCTURE the managerial roles and role relationships?
C. What assumptions will we make about the motivation and problem-solving capabilities of PEOPLE?
D. What cross-organizational managerial PROCESSES will we use to get the work done?
E. What INFORMATION/KNOWLEDGE processing support systems and applications will we use to enhance performance?

Regardless of the primary elements of an architecture (see Figure 6–1), it is most important to recognize the *interdependence* of the factors. In other words, a decision in one domain has an automatic effect on the others. To change one factor without adjusting the others is to put the system out of balance. Decision-making becomes difficult and ineffective. Systematic choices can have a direct impact on the quality and effectiveness of decision-making processes worldwide. In some respects, it may be more important to understand the interrelationship of the factors than the factors themselves.

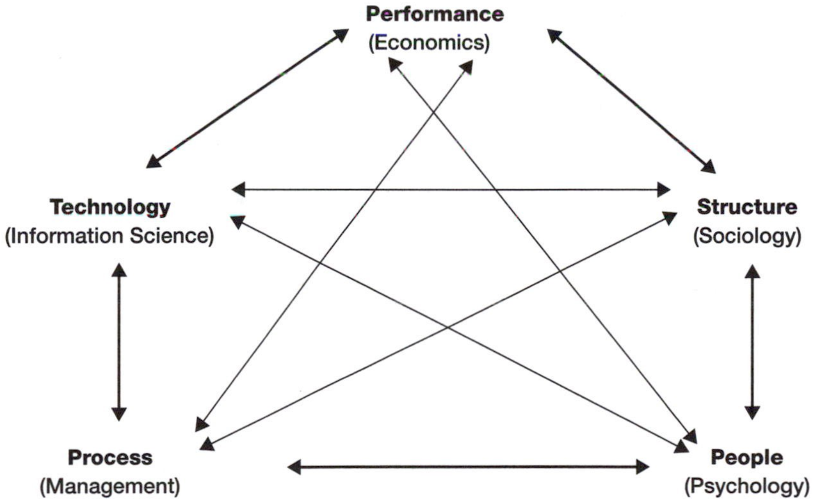

Figure 6–1 System in Balance.

The following examples will illustrate the value of the systems approach:

- The productivity paradox is a prime example of how executives seeking economic returns (i.e., performance) with the investment in information technology (i.e., technology) were not successful because of the behavioral aspects (i.e., structure, people, and technology).
- Companies in economic trouble have initiated major downsizing efforts as a way to turn around the short-term financials of the company without much understanding of the negative impact on the human dimension in terms of corporate morale, reduced creativity and risk-taking, and dysfunctional information and knowledge flow. The results are decreased, not increased, financial performance, and so the downward spiral is set in motion as follow-on downsizing occurs.
- The information technology is seen as an instrument to manage data, not a potential infrastructure for learning and the flow of knowledge. The chief information officer often positions his organization exclusively as being the technical expertise. When viewed in a broader context as a communication network integral to business strategy, the function is perceived as a support/service organization. Then, investments are not made for the wrong reasons and isolated from the real performance metrics of the company.
- The human resource function seizes the learning/leadership agenda on behalf of the company, but fails ro recognize the potential of the information technology infrastructure as integral to real-time learning on the job.

The real problem is one of operational isolation and/or competition for scarce resources, which is precisely what the communities of practice described in chapter 5 are eliminating. To be optimal, the enterprise functions as a system of interconnected actions that should be grounded with a core understanding of corporate values as well as a strategic sense of business purpose, vision, and direction. As organization interfaces include a variety of external relationships, the scope of the enterprise expands. The increasing complexity—operating more as a systems dynamics graphic than a cause-effect diagram—requires that a framework be used to guide resource decision making.

When the architecture was first presented, several questions were attached to each category.[3] They were designed to stimulate discussion, open areas of consideration, and identify areas that might be of common concern. What follows are some of the items for consideration under each management factor:

> *Performance:* Metrics for investments and profitability; asset identification (i.e., financial, technological, and intellectual); qualitative/quantitative success measures; budget level; resource mix; rewards/incentives; tax structures; and creative financing mechanisms.
>
> *Structure:* Learning network of expertise; systems dynamics; reporting relationships; staffing patterns; cultural and cross-cultural aspects; liaison relationships; and collaborative strategy.
>
> *People:* Sense of purpose; work imperatives; individual/organization balance; development plans; learning philosophy; role responsibilities; work design.
>
> *Process:* Simultaneous, parallel activities; cross-fertilization of ideas; cross-functional teaming; global sourcing; benchmarking "best practices"; periodic review and evaluation; and communications strategy.
>
> *Technology:* Electronic infrastructure; intelligence system; service delivery techniques; technology advancements; transformation; shared technology resources; and network management tools.

As David Ulrich, a University of Michigan professor, states: "It isn't important what management architecture you use. What's important is that you do use one!"[4] A "systematic diagnosis" of the organization must underlie effective business strategy.

Connection to the Knowledge Economy

The natural migration from a focus on data to information to knowledge has accelerated the need for management architectures, regardless of the defined elements. Each of the following domains—and there may be several others—are undergoing a major transformation in and of themselves. The architecture is designed to be transnational in scope and provide an opportunity to optimize utilization of resources—*financial, human,* and *technical.*

Knowledge Economics

The shift in orientation to intangible assets will revolutionize the way enterprises are measured. Whether dealing on the level of the enterprise or the nation or society as a whole, there is an entire new way to value economic wealth. Leif Edvinsson, vice president of intellectual resources, has led the way by publishing supplements to the Skandia Annual Report based on the factors of organizational renewal.[5] With a financial tool called the "knowledge navigator," Skandia has devised a way to monitor the intangible assets from business unit to business unit. Subsequently, it has launched new efforts to manage the future as an asset with the Skandia Futures Centers and the supplement dedicated to innovation capital.[6]

For many of today's executives, if it cannot be measured, it is not of value. And yet, as we now understand the productivity paradox, we realize that even intangible factors must be defined, monitored, and evaluated in the knowledge economy. Associations for certified public accountants in several countries have tackled the issue of intangible assets being integral to the functioning of an organization.

Another major factor in the new global knowledge economy is the effect of the removal of trade barriers. In some respects, this has certainly opened the doors for large corporations with an international presence to leverage their capabilities to all corners of the globe. Cross-cultural knowledge, simply because of economies of scale and scope, becomes a competence of a major firm to leverage. On the other hand, John Naisbett, author of *Global Paradox*, contends that "the bigger the world economy, the more powerful its smallest players."[7] In fact, smaller, developing countries may have an advantage to leapfrogging those institutionalized organizations and/or industrialized countries. The smallest performance entity may be the individual entrepreneur, several tens of thousands of which have entered the economy as a result of downsizing efforts.

"What good is knowledge if it is not put to the use of society," pointed out Stoziak, the educator-philosopher in Poland in the 1600s. Traditional methods of accounting fail to track factors of knowledge creation, exchange, and utilization or the value of learning, creativity, organizational change, customer interaction, alliance collaboration, motivation and empowerment of employees, cultural diversity, market/industry/nation transformation, and so on. Until we are better able to determine the key indicators for success, we are hardly in a position to reward certain behavior and, better still, build incentives into the management system that promote real progress. In 1985, Bruce

Kogut suggested that we focus on "economies of experience and learning" rather than economies of scale and scope.[8] Determining the universal measurement metrics to do so is no small task.

> *Primary Challenge:* How do we identify and value the hidden attributes of an organization, a nation, and society as a whole in ways that result in increased wealth for a knowledgeable world?

Knowledge Structures

For fifty years, the divisionalization tactics of Alfred Sloan have served companies well. When a large-scale company the size of a General Motors gets too large, the natural managerial response is to break it up into manageable parts. The concepts of *strategic business units* (SBUs) are still the management style today. More often than not, when new leadership assumes responsibility—whether tapped from inside or outside the firm—SBU's are established as a way to segment the business and monitor performance accountability. What is really needed, however, is the perspective of a *strategic business network* (SBN), which represents more of a dynamic innovation system in which participants are both contributors and learners simultaneously. See Figure 6–2.

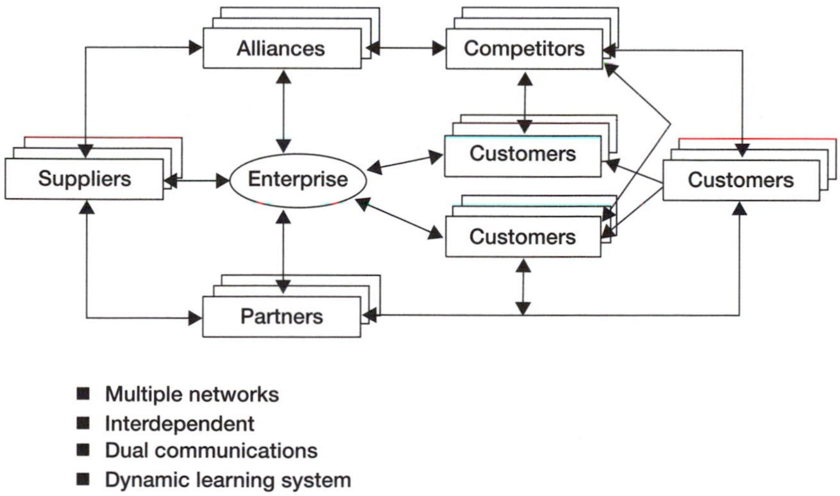

Figure 6–2 Strategic Business Network (SBN).

Some progressive managers have realized that there is strength in interdependence (i.e., the value of the whole in addition to the operations of individual parts). In fact, the "whole" has expanded to include suppliers, alliances, partners, customers, and even competitors. The source of knowledge for all organizations transcends the confines of the organization walls. As organizations develop a deeper commitment to cross-functional teaming, real-time learning, communities of practice, and symbiotic partnering relationships with customers and other stakeholders, the value of human networking will be obvious. These interfaces will become dual communications links in which the wealth of intellectual capital is likely to grow exponentially.

Jessica Lipnack and Jeffrey Stamps have described the context in terms of "holons," which are simultaneously a whole in and of themselves and a part of something larger. As they describe it, the nesting of networks will "accelerate the resurgence of interest in systems theory—both for its human touch and for its scientific approach to management."[9] They cite numerous examples of industries in transition (e.g., Hewlett-Packard, Steelcase, ABB, AT&T, IBM, and Hyatt Hotels, to mention a few) as they put into operation holistic ways to manage the business. Relationships and linkages are the dominant factors in this new era and—by necessity—will be built on the best of what previous hierarchical management systems might have offered.

Those companies that have pioneered in knowledge practices have discovered significant loss of intellectual capital due to the "churn factor" (i.e., people assuming new positions in a given organization), drastic reductions in force from "right-sizing," and the compounding complexity of "training" for new jobs in the workplace. If intellectual capital is the resource to be managed, more sophisticated techniques and practices are necessary to capture, store, and feed forward knowledge to the point of need.

> *Primary Challenge:* How should an organization be structured to take advantage of the intellectual wealth of the organization in ways that balance the needs for optimal individual development and sustained performance of the enterprise as a whole?

Knowledge Workers

When people originally referred to knowledge workers, they were describing those with the skills needed in high-technology industries.

People soon realized that all industries—and, indeed, professions—are high-technology-oriented. If they aren't now, they soon will be. Even the newsletter from my dentist described how he was in the "knowledge business."

Peter F. Drucker, the management philosopher of our time, may have been the first to define the term *knowledge workers*, which he identified as the "new majority."[10] They are considered "colleagues" in both economic and social status, the underlying principle in the communities of practice described earlier in this book.

A true knowledge-intensive organization is composed of self-motivating, empowered workers who know that their knowledge is important to the performance of their organization. Rather than determining status based on hierarchical position, these flexible, mobile employees have a confidence and skill level that may jeopardize traditional definitions of company loyalty. They understand that their knowledge and expertise can be applied along multiple dimensions. In fact, their motivation to contribute to the enterprise may be based on how the knowledge and skill base is utilized, recognized, and rewarded.

Furthermore, developing policies and practices that encourage—not discourage—informal problem-solving and opportunity-identification networks is fundamental to creating a community of knowledge workers. Roles are not to be dictated, but negotiated. Leadership may be as much a function of the professional affiliation as the industry in which the company participates.

Thinking must be "beyond the nine dots," as they say. In other words, individuals and teams are rewarded for creativity and new ideas—not necessarily for performing solely according to the manager's edict. This is why negotiated plans are essential. Responsible risk-taking is desirable, and the concepts of team rewards, peer review, and even 360-degree reviews support communities of practice.

Integration of people planning with business performance demands a careful look at individuals and how they interact. Central to this philosophy, however, is that the individuals have a solid sense of who they are and where they are going. One of the most effective behavioral tools is the precepts of Human Dynamics International espoused by the co-founders, Sandra Seagall and David Horne. In their recently published book on the topic, they outline a self-discovery process in which each member of the group determines his or her predominant personality dynamic.[11] The remainder of their training course focuses on the constructive, productive interaction among people of diverse groups. What constitutes training for capitalizing on the diverse competencies required in the emerging community of knowledge practice is outlined in chapter 4.

> *Primary Challenge*: How does an organization motivate and capitalize on the attributes of knowledge workers in ways that contribute to the overall performance of the enterprise?

Knowledge Processes

The competitive era is long gone. Not that organizations will not continue to compete; they will. But what is more important, they will collaborate to compete.[12] The behaviors that characterized leadership in the previous decade may be the ones that undermine the next. Linkages, crossed-boundaries, and partnering strategies will be increasingly fundamental to business operations and survival.

Perhaps the greatest contribution of the quality community to business management has been the focus on process. Human resource professionals had advocated the importance of process for years; but the quality professionals defined the diversity of business processes necessary for an idea to become a product. Initiatives were called supply chain management, statistical process control, or process reengineering, but activities examine the core process of *innovation*.

For years, we have defined and measured the flow of materials and parts into goods and services. We've become expert at monitoring the flow of funds through activity-based accounting and planned program budgeting. Mechanisms for measuring the flow of knowledge from idea creation to commercialization or deployment are not widely utilized because few have made the innovation process—as it relates to intellectual capital—explicit.

The nature of the process to date has been linear service-delivery models. The systems-dynamic constructs of the future are complex and multidirectional. Not only does the ability to listen (and hear) become important, the ability to learn and share learnings becomes paramount in an organization that leverages intellectual capital.

The intricacies of interaction are multiplied when viewing the strategic business network (SBN) and magnified when viewing the economic nations of the world. In the postwar era of cooperation, it is more essential that nations realize the potential value of regional collaboration. Again, the "holonomy" precept of being both one and a part of something larger is a fundamental concept of prosperity in the next millennium.

Primary Challenge: How is the innovation process (i.e., idea creation and prosperous application) made explicit and measured effectively at all economic levels of society?

Knowledge Processing Technology

Just as the role of the chief information officer (CIO) may have undergone the greatest transformation of all managerial functions, the advancement of the technology itself has been progressing at an exponential rate. Consider the compounding effects of the price/performance metrics; the diversity of media available; the increased utilization, in particular the explosion of the World Wide Web, and growth of electronic commerce; and the catapulted role of technology in business performance.

Brook Manville, director of knowledge management for McKinsey, suggests that the information infrastructure must not focus on collecting and disseminating information, but rather on creating a mechanism for practitioners to reach out to other practitioners."[13] This is the technical support system needed for developing communities of practice.

There has been a significant shift—predicted only a few years ago—from information processing to knowledge processing, which includes the concepts of learning tools, intelligent electronic coaching, decision-making systems, and more. Consumers are beginning to demand more of the information technology itself. Artificial intelligence tools, which only two decades ago were shunned, have been embraced as integral to the successful knowledge-intensive business.

The business case scenario is as follows:

As the marketplace becomes hypercompetitive…

As the performance metrics become more complex and intangible…

As the organization becomes more networked…

As people become more empowered and energized…

As processes become boundaryless,

Enterprises will become *more* reliant on the technology.

Many transformation strategies have failed to include the power of the technology infrastructure as integral to the process. Clearly, technology is now playing a significant role in the internal collaborative knowledge-sharing environment in addition to facilitating the positioning of organizations on the World Wide Web. Information technology managers have become knowledge managers without a full understanding of the knowledge required for business strategy and learning. As will be illustrated in chapter 9, there are ways to expeditiously bring those IT specialists to the task and beyond.

> *Primary Challenge*: How do we define the distinctions between information processing and knowledge processing in a way that takes advantage of technical advancements and optimized intellectual interaction?

The I-Form Organization

There are some significant differences between managing in the traditional hierarchical environment and in the networked organization. The reality is that organizations do not fit into one category or the other; there is really a spectrum of operation ranging from command and control to free enterprise. Some organizations have a hierarchical competence and need to introduce the power of networking to their operations. Others are basically network-competence organizations that require more accountability and responsibility built into the management system.

Figure 6–3 represents some of the differences espoused by Alfred Sloan in his divisionalization of General Motors (i.e., the M-Form—

	"M-Form" (Multidivisional, Hierarchical)	*"I-Form" (Dynamic, Networked)*
Performance	Capital Budgeting by Function or Unit	Profitable Growth; Intangible Assets
Structure	Business Unit Independence (SBU's)	Business Network Interdependence (SBN's)
People	Specialized Functional Skills	Learning Enterprise; Empowerment
Process	Minimized Overlaps; Hierarchical Authority	Cross-Functional Teaming; Knowledge Authority
Technology	Data Processing as Competitive Positioning	Knowledge Processing for Knowledge Creation

Figure 6–3 Contrast in Organizational Forms.

multidivisional form) in contrast to the I-Form (i.e., innovation form) required of a knowledge economy.

Figure 6-3 illustrates how architectural components can be used for a systematic analysis. These are the same components used in the definition of the generations of business management in chapter 2 and in the profiles of customer innovation detailed in chapter 9.

Summary

The dynamics of a global knowledge economy have presented a complexity of variables that cannot be left to serendipity. In order to simplify and understand certain variables, it is advisable that an organization adopt a management architecture to integrate the *economic, behavioral,* and *technological* aspects of the firm. Only through such a diagnosis and management over time can an organization begin to comprehend the integral relationship between people and the performance of the organization. Knowledge being the asset to manage—and all the related intangibles thereof—such a taxonomy of critical success factors is a necessity, not a luxury.

Notes

1. Hiroyuki Itami, *Mobilizing Invisible Assets* (Cambridge, MA: Harvard University Press, 1987), pp. 10–11.
2. Carl F. Cargill, *Information Technology Standardization: Theory, Process, and Organizations* (Bedford, MA: Digital Press, 1989).
3. Debra M. Amidon Rogers, "Modern Research Management: From Technology Transfer to Transformation." Presentation at the Georgia Institute of Technology (1991).
4. David Ulrich, Presentation at the International Strategic Management Conference sponsored by the Strategic Leadership Forum (April 1995).
5. "Visualizing Intellectual Capital in Skandia." "Renewal and Development." "Value-Creating Processes." (1995).
6. "Power of Innovation," Skandia Supplement to the Annual Report (1996).
7. John Naisbett, *Global Paradox* (New York: Avon Books, 1994).
8. Bruce Kogut, "Designing Global Strategies: Comparative and Competitive Value-Added Chains," *Sloan Management Review* 26, no. 4 (1985): 15–27.

9. Jessica Lipnack and Jeffrey Stamps, *The Age of the Network: Organizing Principles for the 21st Century* (Essex Junction, VT: OMNEO. An imprint of Oliver Wight Publications, 1994).
10. Peter F. Drucker, *The New Realities: In Government and Politics, In Economics and Business, In Society and World View* (New York: Harper & Row, 1989).
11. Sandra Seagall and David Horne, *Human Dynamics: A New Framework for Understanding People and Realizing the Potential in Our Organizations* (Cambridge, MA: Pegasus Communications, 1996).
12. Kenneth Preiss, Steven L. Goldman, and Roger N. Nagel, *Cooperate to Compete: Building Agile Business Relationships* (New York: VanNostrand Reinhold, 1996).
13. Brook Manville, "Harvest Your Workers' Knowledge," *Datamation* (July 1996).

7

Knowledge Innovation Assessment—Internal Capabilities

The Situation gives rise to measurements.
Measurements give rise to estimates.
Estimates give rise to analysis.
Analysis gives rise to balancing.
Balance gives rise to triumph.
—R. L. WING TRANSLATION OF SUN TZU[1]

Most organizations have been through the intricacies of TQM, restructuring, and change management initiatives—perhaps more than they would like. However, as painful as they may have been for some enterprises, the benefits (e.g., common training, focus on process, respect for the value of metrics, horizontal integration, etc.) cannot be overlooked; nor can the drawbacks (e.g., reduced creativity, risk aversion, inward versus outward focus, etc.). The challenge for the leadership of any organization—profit or not-for-profit—is to capitalize on the best of the history, heritage, and recent successes in a way that continues the momentum forward toward an uncertain future.

In some respects, organizations are ready to make an appraisal of where they have been and where they are going in the context of multiple aspects of business strategy. With Peter Drucker defining innovation as the one competence needed for the future, the next two chapters offer a systematic framework with which to analyze the capacity of an organization to create and move ideas into practice.

Innovation Assessment as a Whole

Based on several years of management systems research and application of core concepts in a variety of industrial, academic, and government settings, the following ten modules have been identified as one way to calibrate the innovation strategy of an organization. Each is presented with some background material and focus of the area as well as questions to be answered as part of the assessment process.

Collaborative Process	Knowledge Products and Services
Performance Measures	Collaborative Market Penetration
Education and Development	Market Image Campaign
Distributed Learning Network	Leadership Competencies
Intelligence Market Positioning	Communications Technology

Certainly, there may be several others. In fact, for certain industries, others may be more important than the ones identified. However, as a group, they provide a way for a company to gauge the total innovation process, which we will label for simplicity as the 3Cs: *creation, conversion,* and *commercialization.*

The vision is one of *an integrated system of initiatives designed to create the optimal flow of knowledge within and throughout the organization resulting in stakeholder success.*

The value of taking this type of an approach—an innovation snapshot of the entire organization—is one way to step back from the day-to-day operations and even the current multiple initiatives under way and view the details from a distance (i.e., the whole and the interrelationship of the parts).

Specific benefits might include:

- Creates a synergy of shared purpose among a variety of managerial experts across multiple functions, sectors, industries, and geographies.

- Gauges the current competence of an organization against the desired goals for optimal business success.
- Leverages investments made in market research, organizational transformation, advertising, and the use of computer/communications technology.
- Provides a vehicle to observe the management system from idea creation through conversion and ultimate commercialization.
- Enables actionable initiatives for obtaining a prosperous and compelling vision.

The entire *innovation assessment* includes the ten icons represented in Figure 7–1. It is recommended that an innovation team representing the various facets of the innovation process be established to perform the assessment. Through the introduction of the concepts, the collective fact finding, and the strategy formulation, representatives are likely to discover new ways in which their distinctive competencies may be leveraged. Executives who have participated in the process have also discovered creative ways to combine tasks and responsibilities to increase efficiency and/or improve overall effectiveness.

The first five modules, presented in this chapter, represent—for the most part—a series of management responsibilities that are *internal* in nature: coordination of the process, measurement of the process, education/development capability, distributed networking, and competitive positioning. The other five modules, profiled in chapter 8, focus primarily on how the organization interfaces *externally*: new market products and services, collaborative alliances, market image, leadership competencies, and use of cyberspace. All questions are designed to stimulate dialogue about the interdependence of these managerial factors as a way of promoting common goals as opposed to dysfunctional competitive barriers.

The First Five Modules

Collaborative Process

A few progressive companies have identified a senior executive responsible for the innovation process. For the most part, however, the chief executive officer (CEO) is the one ultimately responsible for the overall process. As mentioned in chapter 5, it is advisable to make the innovation process explicit. Once identified as a primary focus, a chief corporate officer ought to be assigned to provide leadership. This is not

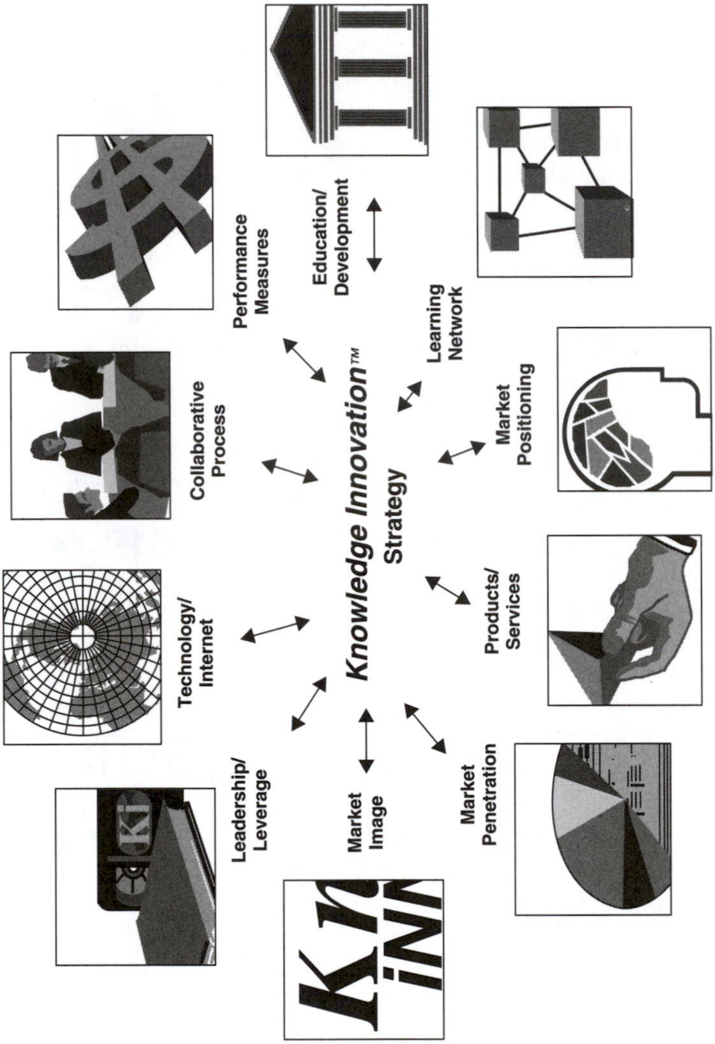

Figure 7–1 Knowledge Innovation™ Strategy. (Knowledge Innovation™ is a trademark of Entovation International. All rights reserved.)

intended to be a hierarchical position necessarily. Rather, someone needs to manage the multiple cross-boundary processes necessary for an optimal system of idea generation through prosperity.

This should be a collaborative process operating as a system of interactions balancing both corporate and local insights. It should include representatives across functions, business units, sectors (if applicable), and geographies. The process should be assessed in alliance with suppliers, distributors, customers, and other partners—all components of the strategic business network (SBN). The boxes are provided to rate, first, the *current* capability, and second, the *desired* capability on a scale of 1 to 10.

Questions for Consideration:

1. Is there *one point of contact* for the overall innovation process? If not, who are the multiple decision-makers?
2. What is the *cross-organizational leadership* support for that person(s) throughout the entire corporation?
3. Is there an *explicit innovation process* from idea creation through prosperous commercialization?
4. Have you allocated the necessary *resources and tools* to ensure efficient operation?
5. Is the *process* a *collaborative* venture or is it top-down and hierarchically driven?
6. Does it include *other stakeholders* in the process (e.g., suppliers, customers, alliance partners)?
7. Have you defined what constitutes *value-added* or success and aligned your business strategy accordingly?

Performance Measures

When Peter Drucker identified innovation as the one competence needed in the future, he was quick to add "and the ability to measure the performance thereof." If there is one place where the traditional forms of management and the modern methodologies come together, it is around the concept of performance. The issue, however, of *what* to measure may be more important—and more difficult—than *how* to measure. If performance is the one place they come together, it is also the one aspect that poses the widest chasm.

The "productivity paradox" helped us all to realize the importance of the behavioral factors, the intangibles, the "soft" metrics that are fundamental to the sustainability of an organization. In fact, organizations must be able to perform systematic audits to gauge their capacity to develop and move ideas expeditiously. It is at the heart of all the focus on cycle time, time to market, simultaneous development, etc. It is suggested that an organization embrace a management architecture conducive to its corporate culture and particular industry. At the least, an architecture should integrate the economic, behavioral, and technological dimensions of the firm.

Steelcase (Grand Rapids, Michigan) adopted an architecture that included the work environment because it is integral to its business and the way it believes workers function in "optimal leadership environments." The Knowledge Management Assessment Tool (KMAT) developed by Arthur Andersen (Chicago, Illinois) and the American Quality and Productivity Center (Houston, Texas) tracks the management of best knowledge practices according to the process itself and the management enablers: leadership, culture, measurement, and technology. Skandia (Stockholm, Sweden) uses its Knowledge Navigator as a way to integrate human capital, structural capital, financial capital, and customer capital. Regardless of the selection of elements, the importance is the relevance to the organization, the consistency in measurements, and the applicability across diverse functions, business units, and geographies.

Questions for Consideration:

1. Is the *business strategy* known and is it clear? Who is responsible for performing the assessment?
2. Are the *performance measures* designed to gauge the qualitative as well as the quantitative indices of the enterprise?
3. Are the measurement systems created as an end or a *means* to promote value in the eyes of the customers and stakeholders?
4. Is the *instrumentation* in place (e.g., metrics, reports, technologies) to ensure proper, consistent calibration over time?
5. Is the measurement process perceived as a punitive (i.e., command-and-control) or *learning activity*?
6. Are there *incentive/reward mechanisms* to promote idea creation, responsible risk-taking, and application into products/services?
7. Have you a means to define and measure the *intangible assets* (i.e., intellectual capital, value of collaboration/interaction, degree of contribution) of the enterprise?

Education and Development

Most medium and large-scale enterprises have extensive education and training facilities. Some companies have even established campus-wide educational centers (e.g., Arthur Andersen's St. Charles Center), leadership institutes (e.g., General Electric, Canadian Imperial Bank of Commerce, General Motors Institute), and even corporate universities (e.g., Motorola University). At the least, there is generally a sophisticated curriculum of offerings for new recruits to middle management and even for new senior executives.

The concept of education has undergone a radical transformation over the past few years, especially as executives have come to see the direct link between learning and business success. The list below contrasts some of these differences; and many organizations, particularly in industry and government, are assigning chief learning officers.

Teacher-oriented	Student-oriented
Curriculum	Process
Schools/Centers	On-site
Scheduled	Real-time
Instruments Measured	Impact Measured
Perceived Expense	Integral Investment
Accumulated Knowledge	Created/Applied Knowledge

The learner, rather than the teacher, is now at the center. Focus is on the process, not the curriculum per se. Education happens not only in structured learning environments such as schools and centers. Rather, learning is a real-time activity that must happen at the point of need and often on the job. Historically, training instruments were measured, but now attempts are made to measure the impact of the learning and how it is applied. Most important, managers begin to see educational allocations as investments in workers' future capabilities rather than as expenses on the balance sheet. How knowledge is created and applied may be more important than what is accumulated.

The concept of an Innovation Institute is one way to scope how an organization might provide a centralized but interdependent research and education facility promoting learning, continuous development of next-generation technology, and the incubation of spin-off businesses. Remember that wonderful high *Idea Quotient* discovered in chapter 5? Only with some form of incubation capability (i.e., a program to nurture good ideas into prosperous ventures) will many of those ideas stand any chance of survival. If managed properly, the educational expense could turn into a profit center spinning off new businesses, taking equity positions in others, and/or mainlining the best back into the company itself.

With this design, the centralized resource could connect with any competitive intelligence (internal and external) capabilities, a distributed network of worldwide innovation centers, and the communications technology for broadcast services. It could be a clearinghouse for an innovation advisory board, innovation fellows, coaching/mentoring, innovation awards, innovation R&D, and a new business incubator.

Questions for Consideration:

1. Where is *knowledge created* in your organization?
2. What vehicles do you have to capture "fugitive" or "tacit" knowledge and *nurture* it for market viability/receptivity?
3. Is your educational/training process teacher- or *learner-centered*? Is it a one-way delivery mechanism or a dynamic dialogue among participants?
4. Does your educational format provide for *diverse methodologies* (e.g., lectures, focus groups, action research, etc.)?
5. Are allocations for education services seen as expenses/costs rather than as *investments in the future* value of the organization?
6. Is learning promoted as an *integral, day-to-day responsibility* of every member of the enterprise? If so, how are learnings captured, tracked, and mainlined into business strategy?
7. Is the expanding *global* economy utilized as a *learning* laboratory (e.g., the value of international travel, cultural diversity, etc.)?

Distributed Learning Network

Consider, for a moment, your worldwide presence. It may consist of R&D laboratories, manufacturing centers, sales offices, service distribution centers, and/or joint market agreements. Perhaps one of the quickest, cost-effective ways to leverage innovation capability is to convert what generally operates as a value chain of functions into a strategic business network (SBN) with all stakeholders serving as both sources of knowledge and points of delivery or execution.

This local, regional, or international infrastructure becomes a distributed learning network in which all stakeholders can participate in the innovation process with local collaboration on issues, business opportunities, and products/services of mutual benefit. What better way to source new ideas and feed them back so they may be incorporated into the business strategy?

Several organizations have recently developed centers of excellence and/or competency centers as a way to concentrate specializations in one given area. Rather than serving in a hub-and-spoke structure, they should all be connected in order to cross-fertilize learnings among all areas. "Network Nirvana," as described by Ray Grenier and George Metes, is "where everything connects and interpolates because everything conforms to approved standards. Everyone has open access to information. Management has the flexibility to add connections or change relationships to match the dynamics of the business."[2]

Core concepts of human systems theory, teaming principles, and organizational learning processes should be applied to optimize the ability to build capabilities and exploit new knowledge. Oftentimes, these decentralized operations are established as independent business enterprises and the learning potential is lost. Moreover, the cross-boundary sourcing potential is suboptimal because operations are perceived as linear rather than as a systems operation. With dynamics changing so dramatically around the world, it is realistic to think that the learnings in Israel may have direct application to some of the issues related to the unification of Germany. Brazil may benefit from understanding the economic models that have proven successful in the People's Republic of China. Understanding the similarities and differences may be fundamental to functioning effectively in a global economy.

Questions for Consideration:

1. Do you have an effective *worldwide presence* (e.g., R&D, manufacturing, application and/or service centers, marketing partners, distributors, etc.)?
2. What is the quantity and quality of *communication* that goes on between centers (e.g., cross-fertilization)?
3. Are the geographic centers designed for "delivery" purposes or to serve as opportunities for *dialogue and learning*?
4. Is there a *common vision* and *shared purpose* among all participants in the "network"?
5. What is the *pay-back* for participation in the network? Is there a way to document the economic wealth of the network?
6. Is the network facilitated by *computer/communications technology*?
7. Have centers of excellence been established in that *complementary competencies* are recognized and leveraged?

Intelligence Market Positioning

Many organizations have established functional responsibilities to track major competitors. In many respects, the competitors are made public on business databases and the Internet. Historically, it was enough to monitor those organizations with whom you divided market share. Conditions such as niche markets, industry consolidation, increased strategic alliances, strategies easy to imitate, sophistication of consumer demand, services becoming the business, hypercompetition, and the like are having dramatic effects on the shape and direction of several markets. Indeed some industries are in such rapid turmoil that it is difficult to know a competitor from an ally…a supplier from a customer. Professor Richard D'Areni, author of *Hypercompetition*, says, "In the future, there will be just two kinds of firms: those who disrupt their markets and those who do not survive the assault."[3]

The information economy was complex and difficult to track. The knowledge economy multiplies the challenge multifold for all the reasons above, plus the acceleration of computer communications technology. Furthermore, mechanisms must project into the future rather than document the past. In short, the market research and analysis done within office walls today will not survive the effects of such an uncertain future.

Companies have embraced forms of scenario planning, which are really action learning models in disguise. The objective is to tap into the knowledge, explicit and tacit, of as many members of the organization and use that collective wisdom—as rudimentary as it may seem—to define a vision forward. When performed effectively, these processes will identify new entrants to the market who may not be perceived as competitors today.

Intelligence will come from everywhere in the organization. There must be more systematic ways for information to be gleaned, value-added through the analysis, and then forwarded to those who need to know. In some respects, the information technology managers who have become knowledge managers may need to be instructed on intelligence capabilities so that they can develop electronic systems to facilitate the process. Also, in the dialogue they may be monitoring in group conferencing, insights may need to be identified and mainlined into the business strategy process.

Questions for Consideration:

1. Do you have mechanisms and systems to deal with the *internal and external* worlds? Are they integrated into your strategy and policies?
2. Is your *range of vision* wide enough to capture signals from diverse competitors (e.g., today's, potential, and ones not yet considered)?

3. Have you defined the new role of the *knowledge manager* as a differentiated or enhanced IT manager?
4. Have you developed techniques for *prioritizing new opportunities* in the context of your business strategy?
5. Are your methods *consistent and systematic* so that insights can be compared and contrasted with validity in the marketplace?
6. Are your intelligence-gathering mechanisms so bounded and channeled that you may disregard critical information from *nontraditional sources*?
7. How is your system linked to the *corporate library/information system* and/or mainlined to the day-to-day operations of everyone in the firm?

Summary

If it wasn't difficult, it wouldn't be worth doing. Trying to develop mechanisms to be able to gauge an innovation capability is very difficult because the process does vary company to company, industry to industry, and country to country. There may be, however, some universal issues/activities that can be assessed even with the very rough scales offered above. On the other hand, treat these categories and the questions within as a beginning of the process. They are intended to stimulate discussion and frame the dialogue among key members of the leadership team who are in a position to establish a coherent, compelling vision. They are a point of departure, not an end in and of themselves.

Notes

1. R. L. Wing, *The Art of Strategy: A Translation of Sun Tzu's Classic "The Art of War"* (New York: A Dolphin Book, Doubleday, 1988).
2. Ray Grenier and George Metes, *Enterprise Networking: Working Together Apart* (Bedford, MA: Digital Press, 1992).
3. Richard D'Areni, *Hypercompetition* (New York: Simon and Schuster).

8

Knowledge Innovation Assessment—External Integration

Intricate Positioning
will appear as a triumph to the multitudes,
But the multitudes will not comprehend it.
Others can comprehend that we have won through Positioning,
But they cannot comprehend that we have won
Through Systematic Positioning.
—R. L. WING TRANSLATION OF SUN TZU[1]

An *internal* assessment of capabilities and competencies is only the beginning. How those strengths are leveraged *externally* is what promotes sustainability whether in a multinational corporation, an international research university, or an independent association, such as the American Association for Retired People (AARP). Whether the motive is for profit, learning, contribution to society, or any combination thereof has no relevance. Economic and societal trends are promoting a sense of interdependence amid the chaos and complexity.

Once again, success of an enterprise may depend on how effectively an organization is able to manage multiple interfaces across a variety of boundaries to optimize results. The value of partnering, capitalizing on external market changes, and the art and science of competitive and collaborative position will become increasingly more important as years progress.

The Second Five Modules

Knowledge Products and Services

In many respects, incremental improvements in new products and services may sustain some industries, but not many. In some respects, this dynamic economy has promoted the notion of change in ways that have led sophisticated customers/clients/consumers to demand innovation in products themselves and methods of delivery and servicing.

To respond, organizations must be able to produce products, software tools, and consulting services that support the value-adding process of applying new ideas efficiently and effectively. Some companies have discovered that what they ordinarily "bundle" into a product or service may be, in actuality, more valuable than the product itself. An international company has the global experience, perspective, and presence that could be quite valuable, for a price, to a medium-sized company seeking to globalize. Companies who have invested in internal electronic mechanisms that effectively create market positioning (e.g., the SABER system of American Airlines) or enable internal knowledge sharing (e.g., the Knowledge Xchange system of Andersen Consulting) would be of value to other organizations deciding to make similar investments. To be able to learn from others' experience (i.e., what works and what doesn't work) is worth a price. Benchmarking, as an activity, formalized this process, but with no price tag attached. Companies with Best Practice competencies are beginning to realize that there may be revenue opportunities in bundling—or in some cases, unbundling—accumulated knowledge and making it available in their portfolio of products and services.

Perhaps the most important thing to realize in determining new knowledge products and services is the potential positioning in the marketplace. For years, organizations have been able to focus on existing market offerings and articulated customer needs. More and more, however, as defined by C. K. Prahalad and Gary Hamel (see Figure 8-1), the real unleashed opportunity may belong to those able to fulfill *unarticulated* customer/client needs and *unserved* markets.[2]

Other management gurus have warned that the way organizations view their future product positioning may be significantly differ-

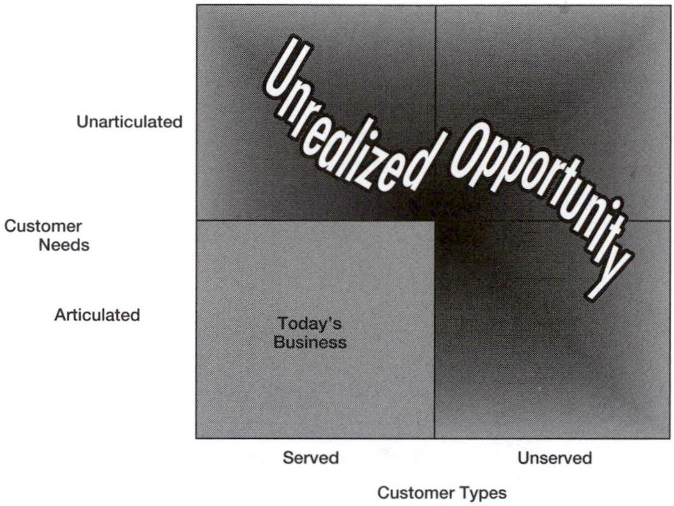

Figure 8–1 Opportunity Matrix. (Source: Gary Hamel and C.K. Prahalad, 1994.)

ent than what they offer today. John Sviokla, a Harvard professor, describes the market*space* rather than the marketplace.[3] He suggests that the traditional seller/buyer interaction has virtually disappeared. Value to the customer gets created in a new value proposition redefined as *content, context,* and *infrastructure*. One prime example of this dramatic change is the fact that the information about the information (i.e., the *T.V. Guide*) may be more profitable than the base television program business itself. We can only imagine a future in which "knowledge about knowledge" will be valued at an exponential rate.

Stan Davis and Jim Botkin have suggested in their *Harvard Business Review* article that knowledge doubles every seven years.[4] That being the case, what students learn in their first year of college may be obsolete by graduation. In the same article they define some of the characteristics for knowledge products, such as they get smarter with use, you get smarter with their use, they adjust to changing circumstance and customize offerings. They have relatively short life cycles and enable customers to act in real-time. Such parameters for product development may become more the norm than the exception as the knowledge economy unfolds.

Questions for Consideration:

1. What *percent* of your products and services are new in a given year? How does this compare to the *norms of your industry*?
2. Do you have the ability to create products and services to meet the *unarticulated* and *unserved needs* of the marketplace ahead of your competition?
3. What are your *unrealized competencies* (i.e., content and process) that might be converted to unique capabilities, packaged, and sold to the marketplace?
4. Are there current products and services being provided to customers that could be *unbundled* and marketed at a premium?
5. Do you have a method to *standardize* some of the current customized services, such that the revenue stream can be optimized?
6. Have you set aside *investment capital* to fund and nurture a percentage of new ideas?
7. Have you applied *knowledge product design principles* (Davis/Botkin) to discover how you might effectively compete in the knowledge economy?

Collaborative Market Penetration

Organizations are awakening to the negative effects of competitive strategy. Not that competition is bad, but in some cases, it can actually cause the reverse effect than that intended. When resources are scarce, fierce competition for precious enterprise resources may be self-defeating. The notions of *collaboration* (i.e., shared strategy and synergistic win/win scenarios) are more powerful than *cooperation* (i.e., balanced power and win/win) or *competition* (i.e., win/lose). Organizations able to manage an array of partner interactions for both learning and economic value are likely to maintain enough flexibility to sustain market changes.

Although alliances between companies have become a major competitive tool, they can, however, be mishandled, waste resources (e.g., money, time, and effort) and have disastrous strategic implications, according to such experts as Larraine Segil in her recently published *Intelligent Business Alliances*.[5] Managing such complex relationships requires foresight and skill in leveraging relationships from which both or all parties benefit.

It may be that an entire new world economic order is now forming and that future measurements may be based on sets of alliances against sets of alliances. Certainly, in any intelligence gathering, the alliances of a given competitor must be analyzed to gain a full perspective of market strength. In addition, an organization can hardly expect to ride the waves of impending market changes without assistance from a variety of partnering relationships—from collaborative R&D to joint marketing relationships and cooperative service distribution channels.

Many companies have recognized the importance of this phenomenon and assigned executives to manage the process and monitor results of the investment. What Segil discovered in her 1989 research was that many Japanese firms cooperate in alliances as a function of learning, not necessarily expecting any economic return. Using alliances as a learning tool is still a concept quite foreign to U.S.-based manufacturers. There are exceptions, especially those who understand the power of action research and customer intimacy. This will be detailed more in chapter 9.

Questions for Consideration:

1. Have you considered alternative *channels of distribution* for your products and services?
2. Is your view of the *enterprise expansive* (i.e., includes stakeholders, partners, customers)?
3. Does your alliance process define *new rules* of participation and *measures* of performance?
4. Have you defined a *map* of your existing network of strategic alliances and made plans for future evolution?
5. Are there methods you employ to *capture the learning* from partner interaction in addition to reaping the traditional economic return on investment?
6. Do you maintain a balance of *cooperative* (i.e., dividing the pie) and *collaborative* (i.e., creating new pies) relationships?
7. Do you have methods to monitor the strategic alliances of your *partners* as well as your *competitors*?

Market Image Campaign

As they say, "You don't get a second chance to make a first impression." How companies are perceived in the marketplace must be integral to their business strategy. An organization needs a comprehensive, integrated communications strategy that leverages its ability to capitalize on its intellectual competence. External messages must be consistent with an organization's culture, vision, and internal competencies.

Over the past year, we have been monitoring the multiplicity of messages used in a variety of media, from company servicemarks to advertisements on television, on radio, and in the business press. There has been a significant increase in the focus on ideas, insight, wisdom, inspiration, thinking, the mind, smartness, genius, brilliance, understanding, and, of course, knowledge. Furthermore, this knowledge focus runs the gamut of industries from a financial investment firm (e.g., *The difference between information and insight.*—Merrill Lynch)[6] to a manufacturer of children's toys (e.g., *Fisher Price Knows.*—Fisher Price)[7] to a pharmaceutical firm (*Knowledge is powerful medicine.*—Eli Lilly).[8]

Some other examples include:

The Collective Wisdom of Executives WorldWide. —The Conference Board (1995 brochures)

Required—Inspired; History is to be made, not reported. —Arthur Andersen (*Wall Street Journal,* January 19, 1995)

We Took Some of Our Best Thinking and Put It into Storage. —Digital (*Wall Street Journal,* January 19, 1995)

Success is a Mind Game. —TAGueuer Swiss Watch Co. (May 1995 ad)

The Fresh Product Idea. —COSTA (company truck)

If you can think it, we can make it. —National Biosciences, Inc. (Science: vol. 268, May 1995)

MRI Intelligent Staffing Solutions. —MRI (*Wall Street Journal,* June 1995)

If you think that you can take your time going to market, think again. —General Electric (*Fortune,* June 1995)

Ordinary data-processing vs. information management. Sight vs. insight. —Unisys (*Fortune,* June 1995)

It's more than a credit card. It's smart money. —Mastercard (*Fortune,* June 1995)

Old Tradition; New Thinking. —Harvard Funds (*Fortune,* June 1995)

Siemens. Precision Thinking. —Siemens (*Fortune,* June 1995)

Insight. Another reason businesses look to Gemini. —Gemini Consulting (*Fortune,* June 1995)

Why success is more about persistence than genius. —GSX Intermodel (*Fortune,* June 1995)

The smarter place to be. —American Stock Exchange (*Fortune,* June 1995)

A brilliant deduction. —Gifts in Kind America (*Fortune,* June 1995)

The Guardian—The Intelligent Choice. —Guardian Investor Services (*Fortune,* June 1995)

Permit us to expand upon the idea of a luxury car. —Chrysler (*Fortune,* July 1995)

Knowledge Is Power. —Fidelity (*Boston Globe,* July 23, 1995)

Understanding comes with time. —Time, Inc. (*Fortune,* July 1995)

Prepare to have that idea shattered. —Hewlett-Packard (*Fortune,* July 1995)

To do battle in the Asian market you need the best intelligence. —ASWJ Weekly (*Wall Street Journal,* August 28, 1995)

The wisdom of 147 years. The imagination of a five year old.— First Unum Life Insurance Company (*Wall Street Journal,* September 18, 1995)

Think. Using only 4 straight lines—and without lifting your pencil—connect all 9 dots. Think again.—Dickstein, Shapiro and Morin LLP (*Wall Street Journal,* September 18, 1995)

Our smart energy network is coming soon to a smart machine near you.—Novell and Utilicorp United Energy One (*Wall Street Journal,* September 18, 1995)

Smart. Bold. Now.—Standard Register (*Wall Street Journal,* September 26, 1995)

Thinkpad—IBM (name of its new laptop, August 9, 1996)

http://www.interknowledge (CNN ad for the Bahamas, November 28, 1995)

Knowledge of the World On-Line—Oracle (CNN ad, November 28, 1995)

The Knowledge to Compete—TelTech (business card)

Mindsource (Internet network bulletin board)

Smart ArtWorks—Trinity Communications, Inc. (Free mousepad advertisement, November 29, 1995)

The Game of Knowledge (TV ad, December 4, 1995)

A smarter way to work.—Steelcase (*Wall Street Journal*, February 6, 1996)

Your dog is smart. —Purina (CNN ad, February 26, 1996)

Travel provides the power of knowledge.—American Express (CNN ad, February 28, 1996)

Similarly, we can observe companies beginning to shift toward this new view of innovation and positioning their firms with the competence Peter Drucker describes. Examples include a range of organizations and industries. Examples follow:

Tradition of creating innovative appliances —Raytheon's Amana (*Fortune*, June 1995)

With innovative solutions, we're helping companies like yours improve operations and increase profits. —CSN International (*Fortune*, June 1995)

The search for innovative medicines —Eli Lilly (*Fortune*, July 1995)

Innovative Transportation Solutions —Courier Dispatcher (automobile sign, August 1995)

Beauty, Innovation, Selection and Service —Jordan's Furniture (radio commercial, August 1995)

Leadership, Innovation, Creativity and Courage —CNN (television advertisement, August 1995)

Building a Better World through Innovative Technology —Hyundai (*Fortune*, August 1995)

Start Doing Extraordinary Things —Texas Instruments (*Wall Street Journal*, August 24, 1995)

To solve the problem, try "out of the box" thinking.... This innovative thinking creates surprisingly effective solutions for our clients.

—Dickstein, Shapiro and Morin, LLP (*Wall Street Journal*, September 18, 1995)

Innovation and Artistry —Handel and Hayden Society (radio commercial, September 22, 1995)

Don't Imitate, Innovate. —Hugo Perfume (Filene's television commercial, October 22, 1995)

The Triumph of Design —Tiffany & Co. (*Wall Street Journal*, November 27, 1995)

The Innovation Web Conference (CNN ad, December 5, 1995)

Innovation + Execution = Exceptional Results—Donaldson, Lufkin & Jenrette (*Wall Street Journal*, January 25, 1996)

Innovative and Informative —New England Home Show (radio commercial, February 20, 1996)

It was about innovation. It was about elegance. It was about service. It was about dependability. It still is. —TransWorld Airlines (CNN ad, February 20, 1996)

Innovation—The Spirit of New England —TechCorp (TV ad, April 1996)

INNOVASIAN—Southeast Asia with experience —Innovasian Travel, Inc. (*Travel & Leisure*, June 1996)

Innovators in Allergy —Marion Merrell Dow, Inc. (1994 poster)

From now on, if you can imagine it, you can manage it. —Informix Software, Inc. (July 10, 1996)

Questions for Consideration:

1. Is your advertising campaign based on your *inherent capabilities* or is it fluff?
2. Do your *culture and competencies* support the marketing messages? Are they defensible?
3. Does your advertising position your *uniqueness* in the marketplace? Does it convey a concurrent balance of who you are and to where you are evolving?
4. Do you understand the difference between a marketing *strategy* (i.e., positioning your purpose and vision) and a *campaign* (i.e., selling a specific product or service)?

5. How are you able to pulse the marketplace for *receptivity to novel ideas* not yet tested in the market or advertised by competitors?
6. Are your advertising messages based on product attributes or the deeper-penetrating *knowledge-based competencies*?
7. How *multifaceted* is your image campaign in order to penetrate existing and potential new markets?

Leadership Competencies

When times are difficult, leadership may be the one thing organizations seek most. It may also be the most difficult to find. Whether we view the organization from a chaos-theory perspective or just realize that the complexity and uncertainty of what we are managing defies interpretation, those who can help clear a path forward are few and far between. Perhaps this is one reason that some exemplary companies have converted their education facilities into Leadership Centers—to nurture the capability firmwide.

Organizations that are likely to succeed will participate visibly in initiatives and forums that seek to advance the state of the *art* and the state of the *practice* of a given field of expertise, industry, or nation. Many leaders in their professional fields may not be leaders within their organizations. They say that one cannot be a prophet in one's own land. Management truism as this is, it may be the one reality that weakens the infrastructure of an organization, rather than making a significant contribution. This is one of the dangers of the communities of practice referenced in chapter 4. This should not be the case, but there is evidence that company loyalty has significantly decreased in consort with increased "right-sizing" activities. If companies are wise enough to capitalize on this cross-boundary commitment to the real work, they are likely to thrive. Otherwise, valuable expertise will readily seek other channels of application.

Likewise, the movement of various initiatives—and the worldwide awareness thereof—demands that organizations make visible their leadership capabilities in ways never considered before. Historically, at least, leadership was not perceived as essential to future market positioning. In a knowledge economy, the more you share, the more that knowledge grows, expands, and opens opportunities before unimaginable. Organizations, then, should package and publish insightful, instructive materials that promote their innovation capabilities (e.g., articles, books, videos, case studies, and/or computer simulations).

The point is to lead, by example, both inside and outside the organization to demonstrate the value-added of innovation and collaboration. Those enterprises that are visible are considered the leaders—valid or not. Even in the good times, many assumed leadership positions in their respective professional societies and organizations "on their own time." There were rarely incentives and rewards to do; and in some instances there may have been repercussions. Today, such initiative must be rewarded, for such activity may be integral to future market positioning.

John Kotter, a Harvard professor, makes distinctions between *management* (i.e., planning and budgeting; organizing and staffing; controlled problem-solving; predicting results) and *leadership* (i.e., vision of the future; aligning people; motivating and inspiring; creating change). In his book, *Leading Change*,[9] he illustrates the necessity to balance both dimensions in an organization. In the system as a whole, there is a need for employees who fit all practices: innovative, entrepreneurial, and bureaucratic. My own bias is that *managers integrate; leaders innovate.*

Questions for Consideration:

1. Can you define a map of your *sphere of influence* within the industry, across sectors, and around the world?
2. Do you have an effective strategy for *disseminating* your knowledge and competencies to the marketplace?
3. Name the *multiple methods of positioning* your own intellectual leadership (e.g., books, videos, professional visibility, participation on committees/commissions, etc.)?
4. How are the *learnings from your participation* fed back into the organization to be used in developing new business strategies?
5. Is there an *internal mechanism* to capture, codify, and feed forward expertise in ways that could enhance the business performance of the organization as a whole?
6. Does the organization perceive *external leadership activities* as integral to the business? How are they leveraged?
7. Are there any *formal mechanisms* to legitimize, encourage, and reward people in imparting knowledge and expertise to others?

Communications Technology

"Organizations will increasingly be regarded as joint human-computer knowledge processing systems," suggested Holsapple and Whinston as early as 1987.[10] Charles C. Holt, professor of management at the University of Texas at Austin, reported on the Crescenzi study of Fortune 500 companies,[11] noting that only 5 out of 30 companies intending to have strategic impacts from their technology investments were successful. "Successful companies had joint organization-technical efforts which involved a high-level management champion and focused upon business goals, evolutionary development, selling, training and team effort.... They dealt explicitly with opposition and avoided changing people, process and tools all at the same time."[12]

Given the dramatic increases in functionality of computer and communications technology as well as usage—illustrated by the explosion of the World Wide Web—companies must develop a strategy of how to leverage the technology on their behalf. They must take full advantage of both the internal and external mechanisms (e.g., groupware, multimedia, and cyberspace) in order to optimize results. Tools and methodologies should be treated as vehicles for increasing the learning capacity of individuals and the organization as well as constituent stakeholders. If we agree with the findings above, the technology strategy must be fully integrated with the strategy to leverage the human capital—more specifically, the knowledge—of all stakeholders in the innovation process.

Out of a two-day intensive workshop of fifty knowledge managers in a major consulting firm, the following roles were identified as essential to bridging the technology strategy with the business imperative. The new knowledge managers should:

Have an understanding of *mission* and *strategy.*

Have an understanding of the scope and depth of the *business/practice.*

Have an understanding of the total *process of innovation.*

Have a *multifaceted skill set* (e.g., proactive, self-initiating, communicative).

Support the *transnational culture* of creativity, responsible risk-taking, and innovative practice.

Keep the process of *knowledge flowing.*

Manage dual processes: *extraction* (i.e., mining the fields) and *diffusion* (i.e., packaging and disseminating nuggets of value).

Provide *leadership* in electronic "stakeholder" interaction.

Serve as the *coaches of the coaches* in collaborative opportunities—both technical and human.

Set the *tone* for the discussion/dialogue.

Document the *benefits* of the "system."

Operate as a premier *global, distributed network* for continuous learning, cross-fertilization of expertise, and synergy.

A focus on technology, then, should cover both the behavioral and technological dimensions of the network and focus on both perspectives: the individual and the organization.

Questions for Consideration:

1. Describe your *current infrastructure*—technical, organizational, and managerial.
2. Is your enterprise aware of the *advancements in technology* (e.g., groupware, data-mining, information audit, multimedia, hypertext, and cyberspace) and flexible enough to capitalize on the expansive benefits thereof?
3. Do you have a *network of expertise* (i.e., knowledge managers or the equivalent) who understand the technology, organization behavior, and the business? Where do people go to seek out knowledgeable assistance?
4. Are the *roles* well defined, the *career paths* developed, and the *incentives*/rewards built into the system to motivate optimal innovation (i.e., ideas to market)?
5. Is the *technology* perceived as an *enabler* to the process, rather than an end in itself? Who initiates projects? How well are they received?
6. How does the technology promote *optimal cross-boundary collaboration*? Is that interaction tracked and measured in terms of value-added contributions?
7. How might the *cyberspace* be designed as a *learning tool* (e.g., information seeking, dialogue, customer interaction) rather than serving only as promotional vehicle?

Strategy Formulation

Now that you have recorded an assessment of the ten major dimensions of innovation strategy, the recordings can be plotted on a radar chart so that you can visualize the current state, what you consider to be the ideal, and the gap analysis, which can be put into a Pareto chart of priorities. Figure 8–2 illustrates an example.

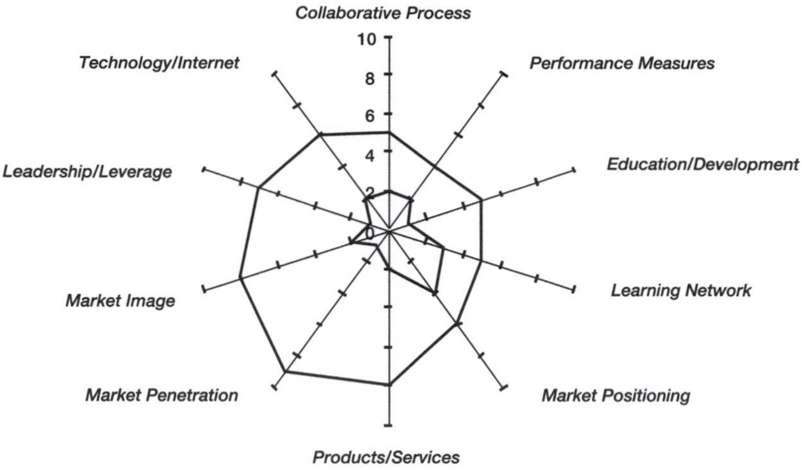

Figure 8-2 Radar Chart—Gap Analysis.

Granted, everyone who completes the questions will have a different perspective of the organization capabilities. In many respects, it is not the number assigned to each category, but the rationale behind each decision. Only through dialogue will executives from across the leadership team begin to discover discrepancies in their paradigms, some of which must be adjusted in order to create a coherent strategy.

Summary

The beauty of viewing the innovation processes as a binding force to bring together respective competencies is the fact that they all share responsibility in one aspect or another. Only with an understanding of the whole and a collective agreement toward a compelling vision will the resources—financial, human, and technical—of an organization be effectively harnessed.

Audits and assessments always seem to conjure up negativity: weaknesses, deficiencies, substandard results, etc. This instrument—on the other hand—is intended to create a process in which participants discover how their capabilities do contribute to the whole. From a meaningful analysis will come increased insight as to unexpected possibilities.

Notes

1. R. L. Wing, *The Art of Strategy: A Translation of Sun Tzu's Classic "The Art of War"* (New York: A Dolphin Book, Doubleday, 1988).
2. Gary Hamel and C. K. Prahalad, "Seeing the Future First," *Fortune* (September 5, 1994).
3. John Sviokla, "Managing in the Marketspace," *Harvard Business Review* (November–December 1994): 142–150.
4. Stan Davis and Jim Botkin, "The Coming of Knowledge-Based Business," *Harvard Business Review* (September–October, 1994).
5. Larraine Segil, *Intelligent Business Alliances* (New York: Random House, 1996).
6. Merrill Lynch advertisement. *Wall Street Journal* (April 4, 1995).
7. Fisher Price television advertisement (December 4, 1996).
8. Eli Lilly advertisement. *Fortune* (July 1995).
9. John Kotter, *Leading Change* (Boston: Harvard Business School Press, 1996).
10. C. Holsapple and A. Whinston, "Knowledge-Based Organizations," *Information Society* 5 (1987): 77–90.
11. A. Crescenzi, "The Dark Side of IS Implementation," *Information Strategy: The Executive's Journal* 5, no. 1 (1988): 20–29.
12. Charles C. Holt, "Organizations and Organizational Support Systems of the Future: Joint Design of Organizations and Computer-Communications-Information Systems," in *ThinkWork: Working, Learning and Managing in a Computer-Interactive Society* (Westport, CT: Praeger Publishers, 1992), p. 39.

9

Customers as a Source of Knowledge

Agile competition demands
that the processes that support
the creation, production and distribution of goods and services
be centered on the customer-perceived value of products.
This is very different
from building a customer-centered company.
—AGILE COMPETITORS[1]

Organizations are beginning to (re)discover the value of the customer at the same time they are (re)discovering their own sense of purpose and position in the marketplace. With today's products and services so readily replicated and made available through a variety of delivery mechanisms, an integral relationship with customers may be essential.

Amid the rigorous execution of restructuring and reengineering, the realization that customers are the raison d'etre for existence has been lost. As described by Britton Manasco, editor of *Knowledge, Inc.*, "We have been far too introspective for far too long...too much time [has been spent] rearranging the furniture in our house and not enough time with the people who enable us to pay the mortgage."[2] Although Quality Function Deployment (QFD) methodologies did attempt to place the customer as the focal point of all company functions, few comprehend the significance of such partnering.

Many companies have established major customer-driven initiatives in order to offset the previous product-driven strategies of the 1980s. To illustrate, consider the following three options:

Approach 1: *Where can we place our products?*

Approach 2: *What do our customers want?*

Approach 3: *What can we do to ensure the profitable growth of our customers?*

Companies who embrace the first approach tend to be *technology-push* companies who believe that if you build a better mousetrap, customers will race to your doorstep. In virtually new markets or less competitive environments and abundant resources, this strategy can work...for a while. However, when resources become constrained and the market becomes hypercompetitive, organizations tend to shift the pendulum in the oppposite direction and become *market-driven*: another strategy that is less than optimal.

Ralph Gomery, former vice president of IBM and now director of the Sloan Foundation, defined the new competitive environment as one of "and" not "either/or" in a 1989 address to the National Conference for the Advancement of Research.[3] Companies must be able to maintain enough flexibility to manage short- and long-term objectives simultaneously. The reality is that dynamic markets demand a *balance* of technology-push and market-pull.

The third approach opens the door to a far more interdependent relationship in which customers are viewed in terms of success rather than satisfaction. This strategic business network (SBN) view of the enterprise includes a perspective on the customer and the customer's customer.

New Customer Intimacy

A focus on customers is nothing new, especially for embryonic companies or enterprises that seem to survive dramatic market shifts in their industry. Indeed, a great deal has been written on concepts of innovation germinating from customer interaction and the lifetime value of a customer. As pointed out by Don Peppers and Martha Rogers, co-authors of *The 1:1 Future*, statistics show that "it is far more profitable to invest in retaining existing customers than devoting most resources to finding new ones."[4] A new form of "relationship marketing" is the best way to develop a continuing business relationship.

To be successful in today's marketplace demands a sense of focus, priorities, and careful resource allocation. In their *New York Times* bestseller,[5] Michael L. Treacy and Fred Wiersema define three potential domains for positioning: operational excellence, product/service leadership, and customer intimacy. They suggest that a company must select and concentrate on the best option for its given competencies. In reality, enterprises must be adept at balancing all three if they are to sustain future market positioning.

Operationally, they must provide for cost, quality, variety, availability, and convenience, and leverage economies of scale, scope, and learning. Leadership in producing new products and services is necessary and usually on a global scale. This requires continuous process improvements, balancing market dynamics, and accelerating the speed to market. Partnering with suppliers and distributors requires more selective integration of policies, processes, and practices than ever before. With the dramatic decreases in product/service life cycles, an effective R&D capability for both products and services is required to enable a steady stream of profitable ideas.

This new or renewed domain of "customer intimacy" is not well defined in the literature and in practice. Later in this chapter, "profiles of innovation" will provide examples of how companies are experimenting with new modes of partnering with customers. Most quality programs have promoted the concept of exceeding expectations and, in some cases, progressive companies have realized that a focus on the customer's customer may reveal a more viable long-term view of the relationship. A few companies in a variety of industries have initiated collaborative mechanisms to define those unarticulated needs and treat customers as potential sources of that knowledge.

Customers have knowledge about your products and services. They also have knowledge of your competitors and their relative capabilities. They may even know more of your competitors' strategic direction than you might glean from a sophisticated competitive intelligence function of your own. More important, they know what they need—or at least what they think they need. They understand their own business challenges and what it takes for their business success. What they do not know—and what can be learned only through concentrated collaboration—is what is possible through an interlacing of their competencies with your own.

The ideal relationship, then, is one of symbiosis in which each is able to contribute to and build on the ideas of the other. Customers—who oftentimes today can also be suppliers, alliance partners, and even competitors simultaneously—are considered stakeholders and are treated accordingly. This collaborative system of interactions benefits most participants and can result in optimal business strategies that will weather the unexpected dynamics of the economy.

Innovating with the Customer

In the IQ^ Transformation project with the Office of Corporate Relations of the Massachusetts Institute of Technology, a careful examination of customer interaction revealed three distinct methods of operation: Sales, Relationship, and Partnership. Current products and services were plotted in a matrix assessing the type of content (i.e., data, information, knowledge, etc.) and the degree of involvement. Figure 9–1 represents a contrast of the mutiple forms of interaction that may be advisable in a given business.

In some instances, the *Sales Model*—a data-intensive, product-push strategy—is ideal to reach a broad base of potential customers or even to provide base services to existing customers. Focus of interaction is traditional, linear, and designed in delivery mode. The *Relationship Model* builds on the concept of value-added for the customer. Resulting marketing programs represent that shift of the pendulum to produce precisely what the market requests. Often, these relationships are the outcome of a total quality program designed to promote customer satisfaction as the metric of best practice and company performance.

Some companies have succeeded based on an institutionalized *Partnership Model,* in which customer interaction is fundamental to the formulation of business strategy. In other words, customer knowledge is instrumental in the development of new products and services to meet potential market demand. For example, several high-technology companies (Digital Equipment, IBM, AT&T) established very sophisticated user societies as a way to understand the real needs of customers and project what future enhancements would help lead the industry. Some consumer-dependent companies (e.g., Corning, Armstrong, etc.) maintain elaborate research centers for customers to provide direct feedback on products and services under development.

Other progressive partner models rely on the concepts of action research and mutual learning environments (e.g., Steelcase, Nortel,

	Sales Model	***Relationship Model***	***Partnership Model***
Vision	Purpose	Mission	Strategic Intent
Strategy	Product-Push	Market-Pull	Balanced Product/Market
Management	Data-Based	Information-Based	Knowledge-Based
Communication	Top Down	Up/Down	Network Learning
Focus	Stove Pipes	Cooperation	Collaboration
Interaction	Traditional	Planned	Symbiotic
Value	Product as Capital	Finance as Capital	Knowledge as Capital
Measure	Customer Retention	Customer Satisfaction	Customer Success

Figure 9–1 Contrast of Models.

Lotus, etc.) as the optimal means to assess unarticulated needs and unserved markets. In this regard, there is a strategic intent to balance what the company may provide and what the market may demand. These collaborative interactions may represent shared risk, networked learning, and symbiosis as a way of creating more together than they ever could have envisioned—never mind achieved—separately. Knowledge and intellectual capital are the assets to be valued, and stakeholder success, including that of customers, is the measure of performance.

This concept—*success versus satisfaction*—represents a dramatic shift in orientation. Many companies are beginning to describe their care, concern, and action in their marketing messages. Similar to the new articulation of knowledge- and innovation-based marketing campaigns, companies are vying for customers through messages of commitment: *Customerize* (Unisys); *Relationships that Endure* (Citibank); *If it's your concern, it's our concern* (Chrysler); *Helping Investors Help Themselves* (Schwab); *Our Business Is Helping Yours* (General Electric Capital Services); *Keeping You Ahead of the Game* (Bell South).

Of course, it is one thing to advertise an emphasis on customer success; it is quite another thing to deliver on such a promise. The first step is to make the goal explicit. The next is to transform the objective into actionable products and services. For years, organizations—including nonprofit associations—have taken a sales approach with a focus on customer *retention*, which is defined in the dictionary as the "power to hold or keep in possession in a fixed state." This is hardly a viable long-term strategy in such a dynamic economy. *Satisfaction* is defined as "fulfillment of needs, expectations, adequate and sufficient." This may be a goal for quality initiatives, but will hardly keep pace with changing market conditions demanding far more than adequacy. Only a *success* orientation—"a favorable result or outcome, realized goals; gains in wealth, fame and rank"—can begin to project a strategic vision to sustain an organziation in the future. *What good are your customers if they are satisfied, but not successful?*

The *Innovation Matrix* illustrates how products and services can be differentiated based on the *content level* (i.e., progression of data to information to knowledge) and the degree of *customer involvement* (i.e., passive to integral). Hubert Saint-Onge, then with the Canadian Imperial Bank of Commerce (CIBC), has used the matrix as a way to differentiate the bank's products and services in the marketplace. See Figure 9–2.

The categories in Figure 9–2 represent the financial industry. However, the same matrix can be used to plot the products and services of any company or any industry. In fact, nonprofit organizations may find the tool of value as they begin to assess the relative importance of current offerings and what might be needed for the future. The matrix illustrates another fundamental principle of success in the new

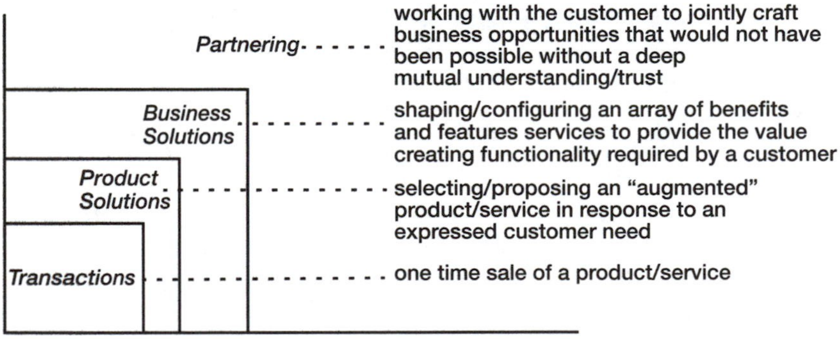

Figure 9–2 Knowledge Capital Dynamics.

knowledge economy. *Mass customization*, well defined by Joe Pine,[6] is the only cost-effective strategy for providing standard and customized services simultaneously. The partnering activities in the upper right quadrant are very costly in terms of the required time and knowledge, as well as finances. However, they represent the only path to efficiently creating a viable future path.

Organizations must allocate investment resources to develop these types of knowedge-intensive partnering programs to ascertain which elements can then be standardized and offered at competitive costs through mass marketing (i.e., data/information-intensive market push).

Knowledge Economy Innovation Twist

How might such a vision be operationalized? There are as many approaches as there are companies. Each industry is different. Every enterprise must determine—based on its company values, culture, resource priorities, and constraints—the appropriate level of customer interaction and methods to mainline knowledge gained through the process back into the formulation of corporate strategy. *Your success is a function of the success of your customer.* With few exceptions, the more your customers realize their own goals, the more reliant they may become on the products and services you offer. If success means growth, they will need more. If success means globalization, they may rely upon your increased international presence. If success means the cure of a disease, their loyalty will increase over time. Sometimes, success may mean less reliance on your products and services. In these cases, it may be essential to use that knowledge to create new businesses required for the future. In short, a success strategy is likely to create new markets—in addition to capturing market share—and will engage employees in ways that can lead to exponential growth.

There are ways to interconnect the innovation cycles of your company and your customers. Of course, the content and labels may change from industry to industry, but basically all enterprises—profit and not-for-profit—experience similar stages in the innovation process. Let us say that the innovation process has seven stages. The cycle generally starts (*Stage I*) with defining a strategy through the discovery of new ideas—whether they are created or acquired. There are steps to identify competitive positioning (*Stage II*), aligning competencies (*Stage III*), and converting materials or ideas into products and services (*Stage IV*). Then, there are marketing and sales programs (*Stage V*) and service delivery (*Stage VI*) activities. The final step (*Stage VII*) is to ensure market penetration and leverage of the original investment dollars. Business results feed the strategies for the next phase of strategic planning.

All types of customers/clients/consumers experience precisely the same innovation cycle, the results feeding their planning process. They undergo the same activities, although not necessarily in a specific order. Their content and strategic objectives may differ, but the similarity in process can be a foundation for mutual success.

Innovation is not a linear process to be sure; but for the purpose of this illustration, we can envision this closed-loop cycle where the business results feed the next planning cycle of a given company. The same planning cycle pertains to your customers. Each can choose to manage the process independently of one another. However, the dynamics of a hypercompetitive economy demand something significantly different from traditional management methods. Not even customer satisfaction initiatives reap the value to be gained with a more integral relationship. It is the "twist" (see Figure 9–3) in the relationship that enables a company to view the success of their customers as their own. This was featured in a newsletter produced in the United Kingdom by Dr. David J. Skyrme.[7]

The symbiotic result is insight and foresight previously unimaginable. This seamless set of interactions, one feeding on the new ideas

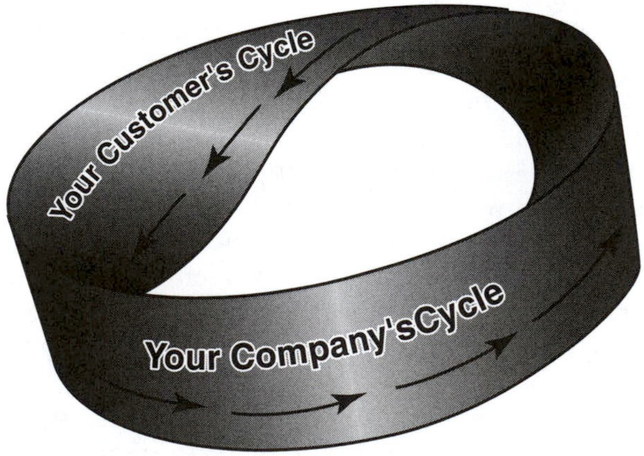

Figure 9–3 Company/Customer Möbius Strip. Your success is a function of your customer's success.

of the other, represents the true value-added of "partnering with" rather than "selling to" customers. These relationships are initially cost-intensive. Companies must determine ways to systematically learn from their customers and standardize when possible and customize when essential and profitable. The continuous driving of new ideas into this innovation system will be the competitive differentiator in the decades ahead. Knowledge of customers becomes fundamental to survival.

Profiles of Customer Innovation

In the recent past, strategies for alliances, technology integration, and/or knowledge management were embryonic. There were few guidelines, no textbooks, scant research, and minimal training available. Today, there are a plethora of services dedicated to enhancing such capabilities. This rapid-learning decade of the 1990s has been enabled by an explosion of computer/communications infrastructure. Executive management learns daily from the successes—and failures—of company experiments. In fact, the learning laboratory is no longer confined to the classroom. Every interaction, both inside and outside the corporation, becomes an opportunity to create and apply new ideas.

Although a customer focus is essential for entrepreneurial niche-vendor firms, many medium-size and large-scale enterprises are finding difficulty practicing these concepts of customer innovation. The simple fact is that it does require thinking differently about your interaction with customers and how you allocate your resources accordingly.

In preparing these examples of building "customer intimacy," we discovered that companies were not eager to share their results. In some respects, they are fearful that competitors may discover valuable information about how they are managing the interaction (i.e., similar to the Japanese protection of process information referenced before). Moreover, they are concerned that customers who do not currently enjoy such an integral relationship will be alienated when they learn about research being performed with others. Nonetheless, every company contacted was, indeed, experimenting. Most had confidential examples of how the interaction actually led to a new competitive product or service. Many had begun to systematize the process with an established innovation office, staff, and initiatives.

By using the following interview guide, we have begun to compile examples of exemplary practices:

Company:
Industry:
Contact:
Scope of Activity:
Details of the Interaction:
  Core Strategy:
  Change Factors:
  Performance Measures:
  Organization Structure:
  People Motivation/Skills:
  Cross-Boundary Processes:
  Information Technology:
Results-to-Date:
Comments:

There are some examples of this customer interface providing significant results to the economic viability of a company. Steelcase, Inc., has for years utilized a practice of field studies as integral to its research base. Dr. Bill Miller is the vice president responsible for research and business development. In this way, insights from the test sites can be mainlined directly into new products and services, and even justify new markets. In fact, there are some who believe that Steelcase may be innovating its entire industry with the integration of physical, social, and informational environments based on action research with customers. There may even be further evidence of the symbiosis in the companies and markets they serve (e.g., customers mainlining the results of Steelcase research).

The core strategy was to create "new-to-the-world product innovation" in response to unmet customer needs and market maturity. Through a co-discovery process, Steelcase and some leading customers serving as research sites were able to ascertain the product and process improvements for Steelcase's Personal Harbor™ workspaces.* The structured research was performed by multidisciplinary teams, includ-

* Personal Harbor™ is a registered trademark of Steelcase North America. All rights reserved.

ing customers, dealers, field sales, and R&D. Their performance focus was on effective work and learning environments leading to stakeholder productivity, project cycle time reduction, and customer success. People were motivated to learn and experiment "with knowledge infrastructure engineering," the label Steelcase has given to the new discipline.

The Steelcase research processes—across separate groups (e.g., suppliers, customers, et al.)—were participatory design mechanisms defined by Erran Carmel and others for mutual reciprocal learning and design by doing.[8] The studies included prototype experimentation with a variety of information technology tools: spacial learning environments with what Steelcase calls "information persistence" (i.e., integrated content/system bulletin board, audio-visual media, ATM, embedded processing technology, smart agents, simulation, visualization, and virtual reality). These concepts—described as fourth-generation R&D—are carefully defined in a Miller article referenced in chapter 2.

Customers are an integral part of the capability building process: (1) concept development, (2) prototype development, (3) internal validation, and (4) external validation. As Dr. Miller says, "You know you have succeeded when the customers think of your research as theirs." Results to date include a 300% reduction in the project cycle time of its customers. Hybritech Inc., a San Diego, California–based subsidiary of Eli Lilly, served as one of the test sites and has documented that the environment enabled their scientists to develop a diagnostic test in a third of the usual time.

Hoechst Celanese named Bruce Wright the business manager of its newly established Office of Innovation in 1990. The mission of the organization was to get more of a business focus for R&D. It did not take long to discover the value of direct customer input and make the innovation office a key connect point into the company for customers. The function—now at a corporate level—has expanded to include remote research centers in Corpus Christi, Texas; Charlotte, North Carolina; and Summit, New Jersey. Since Hoechst Celanese is part of the Hoechst Group based in Germany, the innovation strategy is positioned to become international in scope.

Initially, the task was to review the business portfolio, but the work quickly shifted to the innovation process itself, including the commercialization aspects. Using Cooper's Stage Gate Process[9] developed at McMaster University, Hoescht executives applied classic measures of five key investment criteria: (1) What will it take to make and sell?; (2) Does the technology work?; (3) Can we win?; (4) Will it be worth it? (e.g., potential patents, positioning, etc.); and (5) Why should Hoechst Celanese, as a company, pursue such a strategy?

Hoechst Celanese is also taking a broad perspective of the potential market by targeting ways to change the basis of competition (i.e., breakthrough processes) and totally new-to-the-company businesses (e.g., electronics) in addition to traditional existing product lines. In this regard, the knowledge of the customer is most valuable. By co-creating with current and prospective customers, the company is able to work on existing problems as well as identifying areas of new business opportunity.

The organization structure is one of interdependence among the centers that are called Advanced Technology Group sites (ATGs). The process is one of "learning while you go," through a series of trust-building exercises during which teams of research scientists and customers define, in collaboration, things they want, push for expressed needs, and then pursue unexpressed needs. Establishing the relationship is only the beginning; the real payoff comes later through co-discovery. They are able to glean insights, as a result of the dialogue with customers, that they would otherwise not have had. For example, their work with Hallmark cards has enabled them to better define the technologies needed for the future business of Hallmark.

Their information technology supports the environment with decision-support software, multimedia presentations, and an active computer network. They have created a corporate-wide "idea fund"—a computer sharing device with which employees log in ideas for discussion and get advice from others on the network.

Hoechst Celanese has also expanded the approach to include select competitors in addition to customers. It is sharing insights on how to enter new businesses, how to manage in the environment, and how to develop processes to connect R&D and the business. In this regard, the company is sharing best practices as a way to elevate the state of the business. It has actively promoted internal Leadership Conferences on the topic and participates actively in the Association for Innovation Managers, an organization out of the Center for Creative Leadership in Greensboro, North Carolina.

At Nortel, Inc. (formerly Northern Telecom), the advertising campaign stressed the fact that it is a company dedicated to high customer service standards. Its successful implementation of a new process called Integrated Product Introduction (IPI) has yielded a 42 to 50% reduction in its time-to-market. Nortel's traditional serial process was too time-consuming and outdated. This customized, team-based innovation process includes integral involvement with customers in a five-stage process from design to deployment. Detailed metrics are assigned to each stage and include lead customer identification, customer value-added, highest market/customer business value, achievable customer schedule, and 100% specification compliance.

Cecil Raynor, an assistant vice president, describes the contracting phase as being the most critical in securing partner commitment from all involved. The process is launched with a three-day off-site meeting for visioning, defining current reality, and identifying the gaps and appropriate actions. In this disciplined up-front strategy formulation, Nortel has been able to apply its product design principles to the process itself. With such an intense design and the need for significant trust building, the human factors are more important than the technology itself.

Consulting firms themselves have been quick to establish specialties related to a renewed focus on the customer, such as Bain & Company's Customer Loyalty Practice. McKinsey was recruiting Knowledge Management consultants in 1990. Renaissance Strategy Group and KPMG developed the Balanced Scorecard, which was reported on in the *Harvard Business Review.*[10] It includes perspectives on the customer as well as on learning and innovation and was the outcome of a roundtable of business executives who still meet periodically to provide insight on their progress. Arthur Andersen, together with the American Productivity and Quality Center, has developed a benchmarking capability with an instrument called the Knowledge Management Assessment Tool (KMAT).

Ernst & Young developed a Center for Business Innovation in Boston, Massachusetts, in 1992. Its Knowledge Advantage Conferences in 1994, 1995, and 1996, cosponsored by the Strategic Planning Forum, became a real-time learning tool for launching several research initiatives. Now, for a $40K fee, companies can participate in a wide range of research activities that include Knowledge Transfer; Putting Knowledge into Business Strategy; Knowledge Processes and Work Practices; Knowledge Measures and Controls; Knowledge Tools; Knowledge Creativity and Innovation; and more.

Countries constrained in their natural resources have, by definition, been propelled to provide exceptional customer service. Japanese companies like NEC openly place the customer at the front of the value chain, unlike the management tradition of most U.S.-based firms. The quality and reengineering methodologies repositioned the customer at the center of techniques such as Voice of the Customer and Quality Function Deployment (QFD). Now that the walls of the traditional enterprise have become boundaryless, the knowledge of all stakeholders becomes integral to a successful business.This new value innovation system takes advantage of collaborative insight as a way toward a prosperous future.

Summary

Don't treat the symptoms of the problem; treat the root of the opportunity. There is no substitute for "combined foresight." Market conditions will continue to force increased pressure to provide more for less. Consumer/client/customer sophistication is likely to increase, not decrease. Strategies will be easier to imitate. Enterprises will need all the insight they can glean to sustain competitive positioning. What better source of knowledge can there be than the unique base of customers, who have a direct stake in your own success—and vice versa? Satisfaction inquiries do not provide essential information for successful business strategies. Look beyond the customer point of sale. Customers are a real source of learning and knowledge that may just provide the collaborative advantage needed to compete successfully in the future.

Notes

1. Steven L. Goldman, Roger N. Nagel, and Kenneth Preiss, *Agile Competitors and Virtual Organizations: Strategies for Enriching the Customer* (New York: Van Nostrand Reinhold, 1995).
2. Britton Manasco, "Rediscovering Our Customers and the Knowledge They Possess," *Knowledge Inc.* 1, no. 4 (August 1996).
3. Ralph Gomery, Presentation at the National Conference for the Advancement of Research (NCAR), New Orleans, Louisiana (October 1989).
4. Don Peppers and Martha Rogers, *The 1:1 Future: Building Relationships One Customer at a Time* (New York: Doubleday, 1993).
5. Michael L. Treacy and Fred Wiersema, *The Discipline of Market Leaders: Choose Your Customers, Narrow Your Focus and Dominate Your Market* (Reading, MA: Addison-Wesley Publishing Company, 1995).
6. Joseph Pine, *Mass Customization: The New Frontier in Business Competition* (Boston: Harvard Business School Press, 1993).
7. David J. Skyrme, "Customers—A New Twist on Knowledge Management," *I^3 Update* 5 (Spring 1996).

8. Erran Carmel, Randall D. Whitaker, and Joey F. George, "Participatory Design and Joint Application Design: A TransAtlantic Comparison," *Communications of the ACM* 36, no. 4 (1993): 40-48.
9. Robert G. Cooper, *Winning at New Products* (Reading, MA: Addison-Wesley Publishing Company, 1988).
10. Robert S. Kaplan and David P. Norton, "The Balanced Scorecard—Measures That Drive Performance," *Harvard Business Review* no. 92105 (January–February 1992).

10

Prospectus for the Future

To remain a premier institution requires
that any enterprise be thoroughly engaged
in international activities in science and technology;
it must be a full participant
in the world trade of ideas.

—MIT Study of International Relationships in a Technologically Competitive World[1]

The United Nations was formed to manage political stability around the world. Post World War II, it was realized that an interdependent economic community required an infrastructure to move financial capital around the world. The World Bank and the International Monetary Fund (IMF) were created and continue to play a major role in international trade and development.

We are in the dawn of a new era, one that is based on the concepts of human behavior, learning capability, innovation, and intellectual capital. Knowledge, as the asset to be managed, multiplies as it is shared, unlike the primary resources of previous eras (i.e., land, labor, financial capital).

Alfred P. Sloan's management methods served organizations for almost fifty years. Now all organizations are experiencing radical transformations that require new approaches to management systems.

In many respects, the answers do not exist. The books have yet to be written. The fact is that executives—by their operational and strategic decision making—are "writing" those books daily. The only competitive advantage of the dynamic future is an organization's ability to learn in order to create ideas and move them into the marketplace profitably and expeditiously.

In fact, it is the one capability that is difficult (even impossible) to imitate or even emulate because it is directly related to the human capability. The company's ability to manage knowledge must be at the heart of a strategy to create distinctive competencies and unique market positioning.

Simple Managerial Truths

There are some truths in this new environment that can be used as a foundation for strategic thinking. To many, they will sound foreign—and indeed, they may be. To others, they will appear as common sense—the modi operandi that should have been embraced years ago. The intent of this book was to simplify the messages without making them simplistic, to provide a rationale for adopting an innovation strategy based on the flow of ideas, and to structure the dialogue into the future in ways that will help organizations, nations, and our society take steps forward.

> ***Change:*** The dimensions and dynamics of change are profound. They must be embraced as strategies are defined to ride the turbulent waves of the future. The shifts are radical, continuous, and likely to foster future instability—economically, behaviorally, and technologically. Thus, there is a need for transformation, not transition, strategies characteristic of quality initiatives.
>
> ***Globalization:*** International expansion provides unimaginable opportunities. Regardless of sector, industry, or country, plans must capitalize on the inevitable shifts in economic power and necessities of diversity to meet changing cultural demands.
>
> ***Simultaneity:*** Either/Or strategies are outdated and suboptimal. Organizations must be agile and flexible enough to capitalize on business opportunities as they arise. Matrices of all sorts display this complexity factor and illustrate how managers must create environments that provide for stability and change, management and leadership, long-term and short-term, et al.

Vision: The future is impossible to predict, but that doesn't mean we should not make approximations as to plausible scenarios. Such a vision must be coupled with an understanding of past and present traditions, values, and competencies. There is a need for foresight in all planning activities, but not without enhancing company roots, which include both hindsight and insight.

Leadership: The strategy profession has transformed. People recognize that strategic planning or plans are not as important as the ability to create a shared vision, manage by example, and motivate a critical mass within the organization to commit to new ways of managing the business.

Learning: Education is no longer confined to the classroom. Perhaps it never was. The difference is that, now, performance measures embrace the whole spectrum of the work environment. This applies to training programs, real-time action research, communication systems, and decision-making processes. In some instances, this includes relearning and/or unlearning. Regardless, the capacity to create and apply new ideas will distinguish tomorrow's market leaders. What was considered an expense yesterday will be considered an investment in the future.

Partnering: Boundaries of every dimension will continue to fade. The strategic business network (SBN) provides an expansive view of the enterprise allowing for multiple stakeholder activities (e.g., cross-functional teams, supplier integration, new ventures and alliances, coalitions with competitors). This skill—embryonic in many companies—will become a necessity for twenty-first-century competition.

Technology: Computer and communication systems will continue to accelerate in quality and proliferation. The convergence of technologies and the price/performance curve will help reshape industries in ways that can hardly be predicted today. The electronic marketplace, multimedia, simulations, and conferencing capability will have dramatic effects on how organizations compete.

Architecture: Amid increasing complexity and kaleidoscopic change, organizations will have to adopt mechanisms to manage a path forward. The dimensions are not as important as the process of having a common agreement on the optimal way to proceed. This is a unifying tool to provide some stability and consistency in assessing performance of the tangible and intangible aspects of the business.

Investment: There is a renewed appreciation of the importance of growth in addition to profitability in the sustainable organization of the future. Most organizations have reaped the benefits of quality methodologies and are ready to return to creativity, innovation, and responsible risk as investment strategies. Organizations must reenergize their capacity to generate and implement high-value-added ideas. New economics, particularly as they relate to the intangible assets, are emerging.

Systems: There must be a real-time integration of theory and practice. I once heard someone describe the need for both a dream and a blueprint. There is a need for continued experimentation, but also increased speed with which those ideas are implemented. The value chain must be converted to a *value system* that expands beyond the confines of the organization and leverages resources transnationally if applicable. A new consciousness will blend being and doing, which will have implications for bottom-line results. Motivation (both individual and organizational) will be tied to the business imperative.

Many of the insights above have come from the "intellectual processing" of a variety of major conferences and readings on the topic. Any lack of attribution is certainly unintentional. We are all learning from one another. The beauty of this new knowledge economy is in the value of new ideas—those you create and those you adopt. We are all learning from one another. The more we learn, the higher the quality of the knowledge, both tacit and explicit, we have to share with one another.

Foresight

Take a step into the next millennium.

After several years of collaborative research, a new infrastructure has been created for the World Trade of Ideas. There is worldwide recognition that intellectual capital is the most valuable resource we have to manage as enterprises, nations, and society as a whole There is also agreement that the flow of knowledge will enhance the standard of living in every country around the globe. The Global Innovation Infrastructure (GII) serves as the underpinning for the international network for the creation and application of new ideas.

Germany hosts the World's Fair in the year 2000. Hundreds of theorists and practitioners in the new "community of knowledge practice" convene for a Worldwide Innovation Congress during which economic, behavioral, and technological issues are reconciled and opportunities abound for all who participate. Diversity of heritage is respected, and similarities in mission are discovered. A common language evolves that brings together the foundations of knowledge and the process of innovation in ways never considered before.

Each nation has nominated one person to serve as its representative in the Roundtable for Innovators from Around the World. They meet in a rotunda designed for the dialogue and on the walls is a representation of how their country values knowledge, learning, and the process of innovation. They are distinguished in their fields, but come together to collaborate with one another on how best to preserve and leverage the best innovation practices for the benefit of humankind.

This vision is achievable. The dates, labels, and sponsors may change; but it is inevitable that some event(s) will prompt a worldwide understanding of the real value of intellectual capital and how it can be used to societal advantage. The timeline in Figure 10–1 scopes the work to proceed toward such a vision.

Chapter 4 begins to outline the evolution of ten managerial functions that all seem to be transforming with new values being placed on knowledge, collaboration, and complementary competencies. These ten functions, as disciplines, appear to be converging into a common language. These descriptions provide only a sketch of actual practice. The same evolution could be traced industry to industry and nation to nation.

With the services sector being the fastest-growing sector of many economies of the world, there is a need to establish a collaborative research base to understand these trends systematically. It requires the knowledge of practitioners in the field in consort with some of the leading theorists. If the dialogue is structured and the interaction optimized, there is a possibility that we may be able to establish a solid foundation on which the new infrastructure can be built. Or, in the process, we may discover existing organizations (e.g., the OECD, the

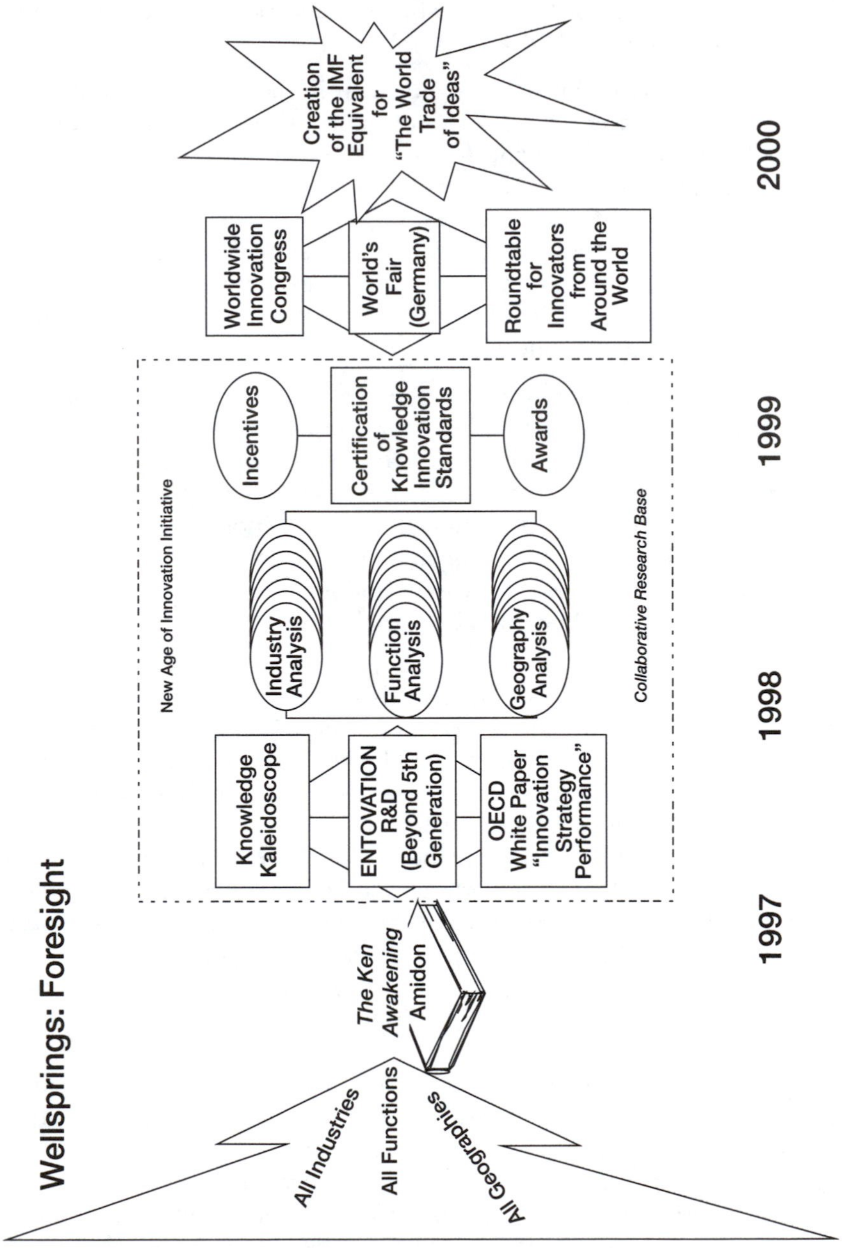

Figure 10–1 Wellsprings Timeline—Foresight.

World Bank, the United Nations, et al.) who are in the best position to assume leadership and/or support the design of something new.

The OECD, for example, has established a new emphasis on human capital. Its previous major documents on innovation and learning and society are two cornerstones for an examination that will now focus on human potential. If OECD is able to view this agenda from the three levels (i.e., enterprise, nation, and society), it could develop new economic indicators with which to calibrate the performance of the intangible assets—the hidden value of a company and a country.

A "Knowledge Kaleidoscope" has been created to track the evolution of the knowledge community and feed forward insights to those who can take advantage. This intelligence mechanism recognizes the kaleidoscopic nature of change (e.g., the interdependence of factors, and path forward being the only opportunity). It values the concept of collective wisdom and shares insights as soon as they are conceived. It operates as a "bank of knowledge" where people's investments feed the base of meaningful information from which all can gain. This knowledge base supports a research foundation, which all functions, industries, and countries can tailor to their own needs and leverage to their advantage.

Toward Modern Managerial Standards

Ultimately, there is enough knowledge gained to be able to define the *modern managerial standards* of the twenty-first century. Incentives can be developed to promote wide adoption and leverage of such standards. International awards—on the scale of the Deming Prize or the Baldrige Awards—will recognize exemplary leadership in the field of knowledge and innovation practice. Based on our research, the following best knowledge practices appear to be emerging:

- Manage the *collaborative innovation process* with a designated chief officer/office.
- Perform *systematic performance measurement*: economic, behavioral, and technological.
- Centralize *research and education facilities* for new business development.
- Establish a *distributed learning network* of innovation centers.
- Incorporate "real-time" intelligence capabilities.
- Create a stream of *value-added products and services.*

- Leverage collaborative innovation practices *with alliances and joint ventures.*
- Design congruent *advertising campaigns* that reflect intellectual competencies.
- Lead by visible example—internally and externally—to *share learnings.*
- Use the cyberspace as an *electronic learning tool* for new ideas.

In short, the world will come to realize a new consciousness based on the values of collaboration, mutual trust, respect for differences, and common commitment to the whole.

Summary

For many readers, this will seem very *impressionistic*, for indeed, it is. For the past decade—and before—managers have laboriously performed financial analysis, statistical quality control, massive restructuring, and the like. They have been so absorbed in the details of the trees, that many have lost sight of the forest. Many have concentrated on the parts without an appreciation of the whole. Linear, value-chain models prevail although their relevance is outdated. Energy has been focused internally at the expense of meaningful interactions with other stakeholders, including customers.

For those of us who believe that there is a new economic world order forming, the new impressions are a breath of fresh air. The concept of adapting to a changing world has been converted to one of innovating our future...together. Claude Monet challenged his profession with his new view of how resources might be utilized. He brought together the natural wonders of nature with his instruments of paint and canvas. He thought grand and in so doing opened a new era for art appreciation. Our own agenda of a society benefiting from the "world trade of ideas" is no less majestic.

Note

1. Eugene B. Skolnikoff et al., *M.I.T. Study of International Relationships in a Technologically Competitive World* (otherwise referred to as the Skolnikoff Report). Released at the "Knowledge Across Borders" conference, MIT, Cambridge, MA, April 1992.

Selected Bibliography

Amidon, Debra M. "Decade of Perspective: Vision for the Technology Transfer Profession," *Journal of the Technology Transfer Society,* Fall 1996.

Amidon, Debra M. "Dialogue with Customers: Secret to Innovation Strategy," *International Journal of Innovation Management.* London, England (inaugural edition; forthcoming).

Argyris, Chris. *On Organizational Learning.* Cambridge, MA: Blackwell Publishers, 1992.

Botkin, James, Dimancescu, Dan, and Stata, Ray. *The Innovators: Rediscovering America's Creative Energy.* New York: Harper & Row, 1984.

Camp, Robert C. *Benchmarking: The Search for Industry Best Practices that Lead to Superior Performance.* Milwaukee, WI: Quality Press, 1989.

David, Paul A. "Knowledge, Property and System Dynamics of Technological Change," *The International Bank for Reconstruction and Development,* 1993.

David, Stan, and Botkin, Jim. "The Coming of Knowledge-Based Business," *Harvard Business Review,* September–October 1994.

Drucker, Peter F. "The Age of Social Transformation," *The Atlantic Monthly,* November 1994.

Drucker, Peter F. *The New Realities: In Government and Politics, In Economics and Business, In Society and World View.* New York: Harper & Row, 1989.

Drucker, Peter F. "The New Society of Organizations," *Harvard Business Review,* September–October 1992.

Edvinsson, Leif, and Buck-Lew, M. "Working Paper on Intellectual Capital for Ernst and Young," 1993.

Forrester, Jay W. *Industrial Dynamics*. Cambridge, MA: MIT Press, 1985.

Gibson, David V., and Rogers, Everett M. *R&D Collaboration on Trial.* Boston, MA: Harvard Business School Press, 1994.

Goldman, Steven L., Nagel, Roger N., and Preiss, Kenneth. *Agile Competitors and Virtual Organizations: Strategies for Enriching the Customer.* New York: Van Nostrand Reinhold, 1995.

Hamel, Gary, and Prahalad, C.K. "Seeing the Future First," *Fortune,* September 5, 1994.

Handy, Charles. *The Age of Paradox*. Boston: Harvard Business School Press, 1989.

Itami, Hiroyuki. *Mobilizing Invisible Assets*. Cambridge, MA: Harvard University Press, 1987.

Jaques, Elliot. *Requisite Organization: The Competitive Edge*. Arlington, VA: SST Ltd., 1988.

Kaplan, Robert S., and Norton, David S. "The Balanced Scorecard—Measures that Drive Performance," *Harvard Business Review,* January–February 1992.

Konno, Noboro, and Nonaka, Ikujiro. *Intellectualizing Capability.* Nihon Keizai Shimbun, 1995.

Kotter, John. *Leading Change*. Cambridge, MA: Harvard University Press, 1996.

Kuhn, Robert Lawrence, ed. *Generating Creativity and Innovation in Large Bureaucracies*. Westport, CT: Quorum Books, 1993.

Leonard-Barton, Dorothy. *Wellsprings of Knowledge: Building and Sustaining Sources of Innovation*. Boston: Harvard Business School Press, 1995.

Lipnack, Jessica, and Stamps, Jeffrey. *The Age of the Network: Organizing Principles for the 21st Century.* Essex Junction, VT: Oliver Wight Publications, 1994.

Lipnack, Jessica, and Stamps, Jeffrey. *The TeamNet Factor: Bringing the Power of Boundary Crossing into the Heart of Your Business.* Essex Junction, VT: Oliver Wight Publications, 1993.

Mintzberg, Henry. *The Rise and Fall of Strategic Planning*. New York: The Free Press, 1994.

Morton, Michael S. Scott. *The Corporation of the 1990's: Information Technology and Organizational Transformation*. New York: Oxford University Press, 1991.

Nonaka, Ikujiro. "The Knowledge-Creating Company," *Harvard Business Review*, November–December 1991.

Peppers, Don, and Rogers, Martha. *The 1:1 Future: Building Relationships One Customer at a Time*. New York: Doubleday, 1993.

Phillips, Fred Young, ed. *Thinkwork: Working, Learning and Managing in a Computer-Intensive Society.* Westport, CT: Praeger Publishers. 1992.

Pinchot, Gifford and Elizabeth. *The End of Bureaucracy and the Rise of the Intelligent Organization*. San Francisco, CA: Berrett-Koehler Publishers, 1994.

Pindur, Wolfgang, et al. "Workforce 2000: The New Management Challenge," *International Review of Strategic Management*, vol. 3 (1992).

Porter, Michael F. *Competitive Advantage: Creating and Sustaining Superior Performance*. New York: The Free Press, 1985.

Preiss, Kenneth, Goldman, Steven L., and Nagel, Roger N. *Cooperate to Compete: Building Agile Business Relationships*. New York: VanNostrand Reinhold, 1996.

Quinn, James Brian. *The Intelligent Enterprise: A Knowledge and Service Based Paradigm for Industry.* New York: The Free Press. 1992.

Quinn, James Brian, ed. *Information Technology in the Services Sector.* Washington, DC: National Academy Press, 1994.

Rapoport, Carla. "Charles Handy Sees the Future." *Fortune*, October 31, 1994.

Rogers, Debra M. Amidon. "Analog Devices Invests in Intellectual Assets. *Knowledge Inc.* vol. 1, no. 2. (June 1996)

———. "The Challenge of 5th Generation R&D: Virtual Learning." *Research-Technology Management, Journal of the Industrial Research Institute* July–August 1996.

———. *Global Innovation Strategy: Creating Value-Added Alliances.* Austin, TX: IC^2, University of Texas, 1989.

———. "Knowledge Innovation: The Common Language," *Journal of Technology Studies*. Epsilon Pi Tau. Fall 1993.

———. "Momentum of Knowledge Management." *Research-Technology Management, Journal of the Industrial Research Institute,* May–June 1996.

———, and Dimancescu, Dan. *Managing the Knowledge Asset into the 21st Century: Focus on Research Consortia.* Cambridge, MA: Technology and Strategy Group, April 1987.

———, and Skyrme, David. "Leveraging Socio-Technological Fusion," *Knowledge/Technology Journal,* Austin, TX: IC^2, University of Texas, Fall 1994.

Rogers, Everett M. *Diffusion of Innovations,* 4th ed. New York: The Free Press, 1995.

Roussel, Philip A., Saad, Kamal N., and Erikson, Tamara J. *Third Generation R&D: Managing the Link to Corporate Strategy.* Boston, MA: Harvard Business School Press, 1991.

Sakaiya, Taichi. *The Knowledge-Value Revolution: A History of the Future.* New York: Kodansha America, Inc., 1991.

Savage, Charles M. *Fifth-Generation Management: Co-creating Through Virtual Enterprising, Dynamic Teaming, and Knowledge Networking.* Newton, MA: Butterworth–Heinemann, 1996.

Schein, Edgar H. *Organizational Culture and Leadership.* San Francisco, CA: Jossey-Bass Publishers, 1992.

Schmitz, Christof, and Zucker, Betty. *Wissen Gewinnt (Knowledge Wins): Knowledge Flow Management.* Austria, 1996.

Segil, Larraine D. *Intelligent Business Alliances.* New York: Random House, 1996.

Senge, Peter M. *The Fifth Discipline: The Art and Practice of the Learning Organization.* New York: Bantam Doubleday Dell Publishing Group, 1990.

Skandia Supplements to the Annual Report: "Visualizing Intellectual Capital" (1993), "Intellectual Capital: Renewal and Development" (1994), "Value-Creating Processes" (1995), and "Power of Innovation" (1996).

Stata, Ray. "Organizational Learning—The Key to Management Innovation," *Sloan Management Review,* Spring 1989.

Stewart, Thomas A. "Brainpower," *Fortune,* June 3, 1991.

Stewart, Thomas A. "Your Company's Most Valuable Asset: Intellectual Capital," *Fortune*, October 3, 1994.

Sveiby, Karl Erik. "The Know-How Company: Strategy Formulation in Knowledge-Intensive Industries," *International Review of Strategic Management*, 1992.

Sveiby, Karl Erik. *The New Organizational Wealth: Managing and Measuring Knowledge-Based Assets*. San Francisco: Berrett-Koehler Publishers (forthcoming).

Sveiby, Karl Erik, and Risling, Anders. *Kunskapsföretaget* (The Know-How Company). Sweden: Liber, 1987.

Taichi, Sakaiya. *The Knowledge Revolution.*

Tatsuno, Sheridan. *Created in Japan: From Imitators to World Class Inovators.* New York: Harper Business-Ballinger, 1990.

Tatsuno, Sheridan. *The Technopolis Strategy: Japan High Technology and the Control of the 21st Century.* Saddle River, NJ: Prentice Hall, 1986.

Tichy, Noel, and Welch, Jack. Control Your Destiny or Someone Else Will. New York: Doubleday, 1995.

Treacy, Michael L., and Wiersema, Fred. *The Discipline of Market Leaders: Choose Your Customers, Narrow Your Focus and Dominate Your Market.* Reading, MA: Addison-Wesley, 1995.

Von Hipple, Eric. *The Sources of Innovation*. New York: Oxford University Press, 1988.

Wenger, Etienne. *Communities of Practice*. Cambridge, England: Cambridge University Press (forthcoming).

Wheatley, Margaret J. *Leadership and the New Science: Learning about Organization from an Orderly Universe*. San Francisco, CA: Berrett-Koehler Publishers, 1992.

Wiig, Karl M. *Expert Systems: A Management Guide*. Geneva, Switzerland: International Labor Office, 1990.

Wiig, Karl M. *A Knowledge Management Framework: Practical Approaches to Managing Knowledge*. Arlington, TX: Schema Press, 1994.

Wing, R. L. *The Art of Strategy: A New Translation of Sun Tzu's Classic "The Art of War."* New York: Doubleday, 1988.

Winslow, Charles D., and Bramer, William L. *FutureWork: Putting Knowledge to Work in the Knowledge Economy.* New York: The Free Press, 1994.

Zuboff, Shoshana. *In the Age of the Smart Machine*. New York: Basic Books, 1988.

Index

Butterworth-Heinemann Business Books . . . for Transforming Business

Beyond Strategic Vision: Effective Corporate Action with Hoshin Planning,
Michael Cowley and Ellen Domb, 0-7506-9843-8

Beyond Time Management: Business with Purpose,
Robert A. Wright, 0-7506-9799-7

The Breakdown of Hierarchy: Communicating in the Evolving Workplace,
Eugene Marlow and Patricia O'Connor Wilson, 0-7056-9746-6

Business and the Feminine Principle: The Untapped Resource,
Carol R. Frenier, 0-7506-9829-2

Cultivating Common Ground: Releasing the Power of Relationships at Work,
Daniel S. Hanson, 0-7506-9832-2

Fifth Generation Management, Co-creating Through Virtual Enterprising, Dynamic Teaming, and Knowledge Networking, Revised Edition,
Charles M. Savage, 0-7506-9701-6

Flight of the Phoenix: Soaring to Success in the 21st Century,
John Whiteside and Sandra Egli, 0-7506-9798-9

Getting a Grip on Tomorrow: Your Guide to Survival and Success in the Changed World of Work,
Mike Johnson, 0-7506-9758-X

The Intelligence Advantage: Organizing for Complexity,
Michael D. McMaster, 0-7506-9792-X

The Knowledge Evolution: Expanding Organizational Intelligence,
Verna Allee, 0-7506-9842-X

Leadership in a Challenging World: A Sacred Journey,
Barbara Shipka, 0-7506-9750-4

Leading from the Heart: Choosing Courage over Fear in the Workplace,
Kay Gilley, 0-7506-9835-7

Learning to Read the Signs: Reclaiming Pragmatism in Business,
F. Byron Nahser, 0-7506-9901-9

Marketing Plans That Work: Targeting Growth and Profitability,
Malcolm H.B. McDonald and Warren J. Keegan, 0-7506-9828-4

A Place to Shine: Emerging from the Shadows at Work,
Daniel S. Hanson, 0-7506-9738-5

Power Partnering: A Strategy for Business Excellence in the 21st Century,
Sean Gadman, 0-7506-9809-8

Resources for the Knowledge-Based Economy Series

Knowledge Management and Organizational Design,
Paul S. Myers, 0-7506-9749-0

Knowledge Management Tools,
Rudy L. Ruggles, III, 0-7506-9849-7

Knowledge in Organizations,
Laurence Prusak, 0-7506-9718-0

The Strategic Management of Intellectual Capital,
David A. Klein, 0-7506-9850-0

Setting the PACE® in Product Development: A Guide to Product And Cycle-time Excellence,
Michael E. McGrath, 0-7506-9789-X

Time to Take Control: The Impact of Change on Corporate Computer Systems,
Tony Johnson, 0-7506-9863-2

The Transformation of Management,
Mike Davidson, 0-7506-9814-4

Who We Could Be at Work, Revised Edition,
Margaret A. Lulic, 0-7506-9739-3

Debra M. Amidon is the founder and chief strategist for Entovation International (Lexington, Massachusetts)—a global innovation research and consulting network, linking forty-four countries throughout the world. Her specialties include knowledge management, learning networks, customer innovation, and enterprise transformation.

Known among her peers as a management pioneer, philosopher, architect, and visionary, Debra has captured the imagination of academic, government, and industrial leaders around the globe. With her seminal conference in 1987 on Managing the Knowledge Assets into the 21st Century, she set in motion what has evolved into an expansive "community of knowledge practice" comprised of theorists and practitioners from diverse functions, sectors, industries, and geographies. Her article "Momentum of Knowledge Management" has been translated into several languages and is available on the World Wide Web.

Prior to creating her company, Debra held various management positions at Digital Equipment Corporation, was assistant secretary of education for the Commonwealth of Massachusetts, founding executive director of the Northeast Consortium of Colleges and Universities in Massachusetts, and the first female dean of Babson College.

Debra holds degrees from Boston University, Columbia University, and MIT, where she was an Alfred P. Sloan Fellow. She can be reached at:

E-mail: debra@entovation.com

URL: http://www.entovation.com